Daily Negations

Daily Negations

A Malcontent's Book of Meditations for Every Interminable Day of the Year

Barbara Lagowski

and

Rick Mumma

A Perigee Book

A Perigee Book
Published by The Berkley Publishing Group
200 Madison Avenue
New York, NY 10016

Copyright © 1996 by Barbara Lagowski and Rick Mumma
Book design by Maureen Troy
Cover design by Joe Lanni
Cover art: Edvard Munch, *The Scream*. National Gallery, Oslo, Norway.
Scala/Art Resource, NY.

First edition: December 1996

Published simultaneously in Canada.

The Putnam Berkley World Wide Web site address is
http://www.berkley.com/berkley

Library of Congress Cataloging-in-Publication Data
Daily negations : a malcontent's book of meditations for every
  interminable day of the year / [compiled by] Barbara Lagowski and
  Rick Mumma.—1st ed.
    p. cm.
  "A Perigee book."
  Includes index.
  ISBN 0-399-51980-7
  1. Quotations, English. 2. Wit and humor. I. Lagowski, Barbara
J. II. Mumma, Rick.
  PN6081.D15 1996
  082—dc20   96-7820
                                                          CIP

Printed in the United States of America

10 9 8 7 6 5 4 3 2 1

For Adam Mumma,
who continues to teach us new ways to say no

Follow Your Misery

❖ ❖ ❖

As the Centers for Disease Control has warned us, this is the era of the meditational. As of this writing, enlightening, illuminating, uniquely nourishing, and empowering sourcebooks exist for nearly every segment of the population, including brides-to-be, ex-husbands-to-be, shopaholics, women who do too much, and women who apparently have little to do beyond reading daily meditations. Still, in this feel-good era characterized by books that "traverse the landscape of the emotions" and "honor the disappointed heart," not one has dared to embrace the largest, grumpiest, and most chronically disappointed audience of all: those of us who have swallowed so many bitter pills that we have actually *become* bitter pills.

To correct that oversight, we give you *Daily Negations*. What are negations? Negations are the negative affirmations that speak eloquently of the ultimate domitability of the human spirit. They are the spiritual sustenance of the cynical, the bromides of the bilious, and the inner truths of the optimistically challenged.

As anyone who's not on antidepressants can tell you, life is not a spiritual journey—it is a one-way toll road to oblivion. It is our hope that *Daily Negations* will be the improperly folded map that gets you there. More than just a parody of easily lampooned affirmations books, each page of this pessimism-affirming guide includes an appropriate daily theme (for instance, "Suicide" on February 11, the date Sylvia Plath knelt on the kitchen floor and put her head in an unlit gas oven), an illuminating quotation for that date ("*If you are of the opinion that the contemplation of suicide is sufficient evidence of a poetic nature, do not forget that actions speak louder than words.*"—Fran Lebowitz), and finally, a transformational daily negation to sustain you through the next interminable twenty-four hours ("Cooking is not necessarily therapeutic.").

Who needs *Daily Negations*? Barney. Kathie Lee. Ron Popiel. Yanni. Willard. Vanna. The Dalai Lama. Tammy Faye Baker. The Olsen Twins. Richard Simmons. Anyone on Prozac. And the millions of pilgrims like us, who set out on the journey to enlightenment only to end up in the real world with lots of baggage and no metaphysical redcap in sight.

Every day, in every way, we are getting older and older. With dire thoughts and bleak reflections for every occasion, every human condition, and every interminable day of the year, painstakingly indexed to save you any further frustration, it is our hope that *Daily Negations* will stand as a paean to the pessimistic, a raison d'etre for realists, and an unfailing source of strength and support to sourpusses everywhere.

Daily Negations

> Great actions are not always true sons
> Of great and mighty resolutions.
>
> —Samuel Butler, *Hudibras*

This morning, legions of otherwise reasonable men and women will be stricken by the misguided idea that today just might be the first day of the rest of their lives. They will be resolving to stop smoking or to adjust their minimum daily requirement of alcohol in accordance with legal statutes. They will be resolving to spend less time basking in the potentially lethal electromagnetic field of the television and more time hovering in the equally hazardous proximity of their families. They will be resolving to lose weight.

By eight this evening, those same people will have absorbed the toxic effects of 4.3 bowl games, swilled something near the national average of 6.1 beers, and inhaled innumerable bags of Doritos. Consumed by guilt over their lack of resolve, they will yell at the kids, kick the dog, and speed to the 7-Eleven for a carton of Marlboros.

Negation:
Why bother?

The margin of error in astrology is plus or minus one hundred percent.

–Calvin Trillin

Having survived the Sturm und Drang of another New Year's Eve, you are no doubt wondering what the fates have in store for you in the coming year. Based on really hard to get knowledge handed down by the ancients (Jeanne Dixon is no spring chicken, you know), we present this painstakingly prepared generic astrological forecast to shed light on your unique and precious life:

The condition of your body will make you wonder about the scientific basis for the theory of evolution. Your oven will need cleaning. Your marriage/committed partnership will not bring you more tremulous joy than the human body can possibly withstand. In July, you will see yourself in a bathing suit and think, curiously, about the sausage stuffers of Bremen. An expensive part on a major home appliance will, in technical terms, "go." When you learn that that particular widget is not under warranty, you will feign surprise. Your children will burst in on you while you are making love and have no reaction to it whatsoever. You will get ill, but probably will not die.

--- *Negation:* ---

I understand that this astrological forecast is for entertainment purposes only, much the same as my brief and wondrous stay on earth.

When a toddler takes an alarm clock apart, it is only the sentimental who can pretend to themselves that he is wanting to find out how it works. Anyone with a longer memory knows that he is murdering it.

–Penelope Gilliatt, *To Wit*

Our earliest power is the power of negation. Imagine you are two, or even twenty-two. (Those terrible twos are murder.) What would you consider to be the correct response to the following routine parental requests?

❖ Take the cat out of your mouth.
❖ Don't play with your food, *eat.*
❖ *Please* sing "Itsy Bitsy Spider" for Grandma.
❖ *Please* be quiet for just one minute so *I* can sing "Itsy Bitsy Spider" to Grandma for you.
❖ I know your laundry has time to visit me. Don't you?

If you answered anything other than an emphatic "NO!" you are dangerously out of touch with your inner child. Go stand in the corner.

Negation:

Today I will get in touch with my inner two-year-old and scream *NO* to the new year.

I can measure the motions of bodies, but I cannot measure human folly.

—*Isaac Newton*

Physicists today can measure the age, density, and viability of a single star twinkling millions of light-years from the earth. Molecular biologists can quantify the billions of base pairs on a single strand of mutant DNA. Yet, in this technologically advanced day and age, no one can measure human folly because no one has devised a tape measure that will reach all the way around Rush Limbaugh's head.

Isaac Newton was born on this date in 1642.

Negation:

When an apple falls from a tree, that is gravity. When a rotten-to-the-core talk show host falls from a tree, that is levity.

If we're moving into the information age, don't we have to figure out how to carry the poor with us? . . . I'm just tossing this out . . . but maybe we need a tax credit for the poorest Americans to buy a laptop.

> —Newt Gingrich in a speech to the House Ways and Means Committee,
> January 5, 1995

We're just tossing this out, but maybe we'd need some safeguards written into the bill to make sure that the poorest Americans didn't trade in their government-subsidized Powerbook for a year of school lunches or a trip to the doctor. You know how *those* people are.

Negation:
I am majority-whipped.

Why me? Why me?

—Nancy Kerrigan, January 6, 1994

Why not me? As the oft-quoted gridiron despot Vince Lombardi said, winning *is* the only thing, and on this unforgettable date in 1994, Tonya Harding, a simple girl with a gun rack and a dream, literally beat a path to the National Championship by landing the first technically perfect gilooley . . . to her competitor's patella.

Negation:
Today I will remember the golden rule and gilooley others as I would have them gilooley me.

After you retire, there ain't but one big event left.

> –Florida State University football coach Bobby Bowden on being asked
> about his retirement plans after winning the Orange Bowl and the Na-
> tional Championship in January 1994

The bad news is that work expands in adverse proportion to obliterate the hours that remain in your day. The worse news is that retirement expands in adverse proportion to obliterate the hours that remain in your life.

Negation:
If hard work doesn't kill me, retirement definitely will.

I'm all shook up . . .

–President George Bush, Tokyo, 1/8/1991

George Bush never did spew out the right answer to an indigestible federal deficit. And a credible response to Iran-Contra just seemed to stick in his throat. But by vomiting into the lap of the Japanese Prime Minister on this date in 1991, George Bush collapsed onto the perfect way to commemorate the 56th anniversary of Elvis Presley's birth. Despite reports to the contrary, it wasn't any messier than the wretched refuse that collects along the gates of Graceland.

Negation:

I ate it up and spit it out...I did it my way.

When the President does it, that means that it is not illegal.
—Richard Milhous Nixon

And when obituary writers gloss over it, that means it never happened, right? Richard ("I would have made a good Pope") Nixon, who proved to be more immune to the slings and arrows of his millions of political enemies than he was to a bubble in his bloodstream, was born on this date in 1913.

───── *Negation:* ─────
Immunity is a delusion.

The meek shall inherit the earth, but not its mineral rights.
                                                    —J. Paul Getty

On January 10, 1901, The Spindletop Claim near Beaumont, Texas, owned by Anthony F. Lucas blew in, thus begetting the modern oil industry. The first oil strike in America's then-largest state provided generously for those Texans not known for their meekness. They got ten-gallon hats for their half-gallon heads and steer horns for the fronts of their Cadillacs.

What did the meek inherit? The tax burden and a few tornado-prone mobile home parks along the Gulf.

Negation:
Blessed are the poor in spirit, because poor "in spirit" doesn't count.

The moral flabbiness born of the bitch-goddess SUC-
CESS. That—with the squalid cash interpretation put on
the word success—is our national disease.
                              —William James in a letter to H. G. Wells

William James was born on this date in 1842. Since he's
best known for penning the "sleeper best-seller" (actually, it's a coma) *The Varieties of Religious Experience*,
we're supposed to believe that he worshipped at the feet
of religion rather than the immaculately pedicured toot-
sies of the monetary bitch-goddess.

James was not only a rich man, he was a rich *writer*
from a family of famous rich writers. Telling *us* that we
should scorn success is not unlike Leona Helmsley telling
us "little people" that we should pay our taxes. If royalty
checks make us miserable and morally flabby, that'll just
be our cross to bear.

Negation:
You can never be too rich or too morally flabby.

I am convinced that we have a degree of delight, and that
no small one, in the real misfortunes of others.
                              –Edmund Burke, *On the Sublime and the Beautiful*

Leave it to the vonderful *Volk* who brought us *Angst,
Sturm und Drang*, the universally understood crowd
rouser *Achtung*, and a million other words that make
hocking a fur ball sound melodious, to give us today's
mot juste.

German/English dictionaries strain to define *Schadenfreude* as "malicious pleasure" or "joy in others' misfortunes." Those definitions come close. But the essence of
Schadenfreude is more like the essence of, say, *Blitzkrieg*.
It has to be experienced to be understood.

So here's a little exercise for Edmund Burke's birthday
(1729). When you hear laughter today, and you will, creep
a little closer to its source. Are those happy people simply overcome with the joy of being truly alive? Not likely.
Are they sharing a laugh over some cutting-edge seventies humor they saw on *Saturday Night Live*? Not possible. Are they laughing at *you*? Bingo.

─────────── *Negation:* ───────────
*For what do we live, but to make sport for our neighbors, and laugh at
them in our turn?* (Jane Austen, *Pride and Prejudice*)

Wʜᴇɴ you go into court you are putting your faith into the hands of twelve people who weren't smart enough to get out of jury duty.

—Norm Crosby

On this date in 1994, a mistrial was declared when Erik Menendez's jury remained hopelessly deadlocked after nineteen days of deliberation.

Before you get the impression that, given a shotgun, a really good toupee, and a Porsche-buying spree, you, too, might lay your inner demons to rest, it would be wise to consider the salt-of-the-earth types who have the time and requisite lack of interest to make up a jury of your "peers." They include: Precious Moments collectors. Women who knit colorful covers for toilet paper rolls. Crimean War reenactors. Those who read—and believe—the *National Enquirer*. Those who write for the *National Enquirer*. Nuns. Happy Louie and his orchestra. People who exhibit too keen an interest in the relative freshness of roadkill. Susan Powter. Humanoids who claim to have been physically examined—or worse—by visitors from other planets. People who, when asked to enumerate their most poignant memories, list their teeth.

Negation:
I will jaywalk with caution.

Technological progress has merely provided us with a more efficient means of going backward.

—Aldous Huxley

Or, more efficient still, going absolutely nowhere.

On January 14, 1914, Henry Ford fired up his first assembly line. Production time dropped immediately from twelve and a half hours to ninety-three minutes per car. Within minutes, the first of many traffic jams (which ultimately necessitated the invention of the car phone) formed at the Ford factory gate.

Negation:
I'm going nowhere fast.

Fashion is a form of ugliness so intolerable that we have to alter it every six months.

—Oscar Wilde

Not on the haute couture fashion show A-list? No problem. Just pull last year's lapels over your eyes, imagine trick or treat night at the Kate Moss Eating Disorders Clinic, and it's the next best thing to being there.

Still, if fashion has an upside, it is that it usually covers the backsides of those people whose nether regions do not bear up under close inspection, much the same way a festively tasseled bunting might drape the business end of a circus elephant. And for that we can all be truly grateful.

Negation:

Now that we have the Wonderbra, can the MiracleJock be far behind?

Good-bye, John. You were God's worst enemy. You
were Hell's best friend. I hate you with a perfect hatred.
                    —Billy Sunday's funeral oration over John Barleycorn, 1/16/1920

This seems like the usual better-you-than-me-sucker
funeral fare until you realize that billfold-thumper and
Jimmy Swaggart-prototype Billy Sunday was intemperately eulogizing a whiskey bottle. A whiskey bottle!
Meanwhile the poor slob that emptied it was probably
being chucked into some potter's field without so much
as a tootle-oo.

On this day in 1920, the enforcement of Prohibition
went into effect after two thirds of the Congress and
three quarters of the state legislatures agreed to ban
John Barleycorn and Jack Daniel's and Johnnie Walker
and Jim Beam from these self-righteous shores. In the
1970s, we couldn't get that kind of majority to agree that
women were equal to men.

Negation:
I won't trust the majority.

My obstetrician was so dumb that when I gave birth he forgot to cut the cord. For a year that kid followed me *everywhere*. It was like having a dog on a leash.

—Joan Rivers

The most famous pair of congenitally linked Siamese twins (Save your postage. Politically correct or not, their mother was certifiably Siamese.), Chang and Eng, died on this date in 1874. Joined, mid-chest, by a band of cartilage about six inches in length, Chang and Eng were nevertheless able to stretch their potential to the fullest.

At a very young age, the twins taught themselves to swim with what onlookers described as "admirable co-ordination." (Reports are mixed as to their mastery of springboard diving.) They also ran in Rockette-like unison—straight to the offices of the traveling curiosity show promoters who made them world-famous oddities.

But Chang and Eng weren't content to be the Doublemint Twins of the Believe-It-Or-Not set. In 1843, they married two young sisters from Wilkesboro, North Carolina, in a double wedding that tugged at the heart-strings—and put considerable strain on that cartilage. Though the twins visited each of the wives in turn only every three days, the marriages produced twenty-one children and some very strange laundry.

Chang died of a stroke at age sixty-two. Eng died of fright a half hour later.

Negation:
I want to be alone.

Words, words, mere words, no matter from the heart.
—William Shakespeare, *Troilus and Cressida*

Peter Mark Roget, patron saint of college thesis writers, was born on January 18, 1779. Today we'll attempt to save you some time in your day-to-day dealings with the outside world by giving you a list of terms. If you hear any of these words in a sentence, you can safely ignore anything else the speaker has to say without missing any real information: proactive, empowerment, agenda, strategic planning, operating efficiencies, workflow, feedback, networking, dialoguing, prioritizing, codependent, state-of-the-art, productivity, downsizing (don't you feel your brain downsizing already?), postmodern, postindustrial, survivor (in any but the most literal sense), wellness, holistic, natural (regarding any commercial product), bottom line, benchmark, interface, accountability, and the ever-popular dis-ease.

This lexicographical inventorialization is structured in accordance with purely theoretical, externally imposed parameters. It is, as a result, necessarily subcomprehensive in format. But we know you get the idea.

Negation:

I will facilitate my interfacial encounters with importantized communications disseminators by telling them, proactively, to deploy it from their rear catchment areas.

The well-dressed man still doffs his hat.
— 1985 Brooks Brothers advertisement

Particularly if he's in the presence of a real stickler for protocol, as was Vlad Dracula, fifteenth-century prince of Wallachia (Romania).

Unlike Bram Stoker's fictional vampire, the historical Dracula simply had no time for such niceties as sucking blood and developing emotional attachments to his victims. If he had, he never would have been able to boil, impale, disembowel, burn alive, and hack to pieces an estimated fifty to one hundred thousand people in his desperately overachieving six-year reign.

What's all of this got to do with the relatively bloodless celebration of Hat Day? Vlad Dracula aspired to be the Miss Manners of the rack-and-wheel set. When two Genoese ambassadors refused to remove their hats in his presence, he had their jaunty chapeaux nailed to their heads.

One can only wonder at what would have happened if they had neglected to lay their napkins in their laps.

Negation:
Here's your hat. What's your hurry?

It is often pleasant to stone a martyr, no matter how much we admire him.

–John Barth

Although religion is the professional sports industry's main competitor for your Sunday entertainment dollar, today is the day to remember St. Sebastian, martyred patron saint of athletes. If St. Sebastian's stats were laid out on a bubble-gum card, you would know that he survived the piercing wounds of arrows only to die soon afterward from a stoning. Today's *professional* athletes can't even survive a Grand-Slam breakfast at Denny's.

Still, there is a small group of dedicated, talented men and token women who will risk concussions and anterior cruciate ligament injuries just to give us the opportunity to do "the wave": collegiate athletes. You won't find them niggling over a no-trade clause. Hell, their professors can't even find them in remedial English class. And you won't hear them moaning and groaning about some lucrative endorsement they've lost. All they want is a stooge to take their tests for them and the honor of bringing a CarQuest Bowl trophy back to their beloved alma mater.

Negation:

If I remember who won this year's CarQuest Bowl, I'll make a memo to myself to get a life.

All kings is mostly rapscallions.

         —Mark Twain, *The Adventures of Huckleberry Finn*

A black day for monarchists. In France, a country that prides itself on its revolting peasants, King Louis XVI was guillotined on this date in 1793. On January 21, 1936, Edward VIII was proclaimed king of England only to trade his uneasy crown for the notoriously easy Wallis Simpson before the year was over. In the third week of January 1981, Lady Diana Spencer thought she had the world on a string when she accepted a dutiful proposal of marriage from heir to the throne and a feminine-hygiene-product-wanna-be, Chuck Windsor. Last and probably least, in January of 1992, a set of photographs featuring the buxom Sarah Ferguson cavorting with a Texas millionaire made their way onto the Buckingham Palace breakfast table, thus ruining eggs sunny-side up for the Royal Family forever.

Negation:
Inbreeding is not better than no breeding at all.

I stood
Among them, but not of them; in a shroud
Of thoughts which were not their thoughts.
                    —Lord Byron, *Childe Harold's Pilgrimage*

Some people look at Cindy Crawford and see the potential for beauty in all of humanity. You see a nodular growth of suspicious coloration measuring more than one eighth of an inch in diameter. Other people look at the starry sky and see a million points of light. You see the last vestige of Skylab, hurtling through space toward the $4,000 deck you just banged the last nail into.

That's the beauty of being negative in an optimistic time and place. The standing apart. The feeling not only that your thoughts are different and yours alone, but that you are the only one who is thinking at all.

Lord George Gordon Byron, who looked at the gorgeous human mosaic and saw a problem that was clearly beyond the local tile guy, was born on this date in 1788.

— Negation: —
You talkin' to *me*?

The only reason in the world to have money, is to tell any S.O.B. in the world to go to hell.

–Humphrey Bogart

In modern parlance, this is known as F-You Money. Unfortunately, the only people who tend to accumulate enough moolah to tell the blood-sucking, bottom-feeding dictatorial S.O.B.'s where to go tend to be the S.O.B.'s themselves.

Negation:

I don't even have enough money to tell my boss to go to heck.

There's no such thing as old age, there is only sorrow.
    –Edith Wharton, *A Backward Glance*

As grueling and ungratifying as your life is now, one day things will get so bad that you will actually miss having a pointless and unrewarding job to go to, premenstrual bloating, stepping barefooted on the odd piece of Lego, and being hormonally viable enough to grow a pimple.

Edith Wharton, who enjoyed seventy-six years of life and seventy-six years of sadness, was born on this date in 1862.

Negation:
I am sad.

> The best-laid schemes o' mice an' men
> > Gang aft agley;
> And leave us nought but grief and pain
> > For promised joy.
>
> —Robert Burns, *To a Mouse*

Once upon a time, you believed that Walt Disney turned a scratch-pad doodle of vermin into a discreetly clothed, endlessly enchanting *real* mouse. No wonder you thought you could do the same with those exciting plans for adulthood you sketched out and wadded up in your mind. Well, surprise, you're not an astronaut! You're not Julie Andrews tromping invulnerably over federally protected land with a troupe of diabetes-inducing yodeling children. You're not even Gidget.

Robert Burns was born on this day in 1759. He wanted to be a bagpiper and proctologist. (Same tools.) Now he's peat.

Negation:
My plans have gone aft agley.

> With the farming of a verse
> Make a vineyard of the curse,
> Sing of human unsuccess
> In a rapture of distress
> —W. H. Auden, *In Memory of W. B. Yeats*

When William Butler Yeats died on this date in the curséd year of 1939, he drew a twelve-stanza rapture of distress from the pen of Wystan Hugh Auden. Shortly thereafter, poetry itself went to the boneyard. So don't expect anything other than a rote recitation of the Twenty-third Psalm at your own passing. And don't expect to hear any curses that don't involve variations of the same four-letter word.

Negation:
Fuck me.

Anything that won't sell, I don't want to invent.
—Thomas Alva Edison

That sheds a little light on the subject of "pure" science, doesn't it? Scientists aren't exempt from the universal desire for a nice comfortable rut to live in until they're ready for the grave. And, as Thomas Edison himself points out, there's nothing like the thrill of discovery ... especially if what you're discovering is a wad in the bank.

So today, consider the purely scientific motives of Thomas Edison, who, on this date in 1880, patented his incandescent lightbulb. His goal was not to add light to our lives (GE and Debby Boone couldn't even do that), but to add weight to his pockets.

Negation:
Turn out the lights, the party's over.

Socially he was a real jerk. Very unpleasant to be around. Very stupid . . . and he always got completely drunk, and he made a point of behaving badly to everyone . . . he was a star painter alright, but that's no reason to pretend he was a pleasant person . . . I'll tell you what kind of a person he was. He would go over to a black person and say, "How do you like your skin color?" or he'd ask a homosexual, "Sucked any cocks lately?"

—*Larry Rivers on Jackson Pollock*

Say what you will about Jackson Pollock (clearly, people do); he didn't just make art, he *lived* it. The paintings that made him rich were mainly drips, and apparently so was he.

Death-of-the-party Jackson Pollock was born in 1912; we love his paintings. Or maybe we just love the fact that he got away with it.

----------- *Negation:* -----------
An artistic temperament can sometimes be successfully treated with a good dewormer.

Nobody has a boring life when you get down to it. Isn't your own existence much more interesting than anyone else's? Look in the mirror and see yourself in a whole different light. It will all happen to you eventually: divorce, complicated operations, addictions of one sort or another, even death. It's lonely at the bottom as well as the top. You're a big celebrity, and you never even realized it. Go tell somebody. *Quickly.*

—John Waters, *Crackpot*

But don't dribble on to just *anybody* about the urological quirks and unresolved feelings for draught animals that make you special. Call the imitable-in-every-time-slot Oprah and tell her it's time for your five minutes (Andy Warhol was much too generous) in the spotlight.

Oprah Winfrey—the real secret to Deepak Chopra's tiresome longevity and *your* last chance for turning that ugly divorce, leaky breast implant, and unmatched set of emotional baggage into a Louis Vuitton full of cold, hard cash—coasted into existence on this date in 1954, pulling two Radio Flyers full of flab behind her.

Negation:

I have nothing to plug.

It's ridiculous to call this an industry. This is not. This is rat eat rat, dog eat dog. I'll kill 'em, and I'm going to kill 'em before they kill me. You're talking about the American way of survival of the fittest.

—McDonald's founder Ray Kroc

Actually, the generally accepted version is people eat cows, unless Ray was inadvertently letting the cat out of the bag about the ingredients in his "secret sauce."

Of course, these days any mention of "survival of the fittest" is as politically incorrect as a superheated, caffeinated, polystyrene-packaged, take-out beverage, but among those of us involved in the day-to-day struggle to maintain a position in the modern corporate food chain, it's just common knowledge.

Negation:
Sacred cows make great hamburgers.

He that dies pays all debts.

−William Shakespeare, The Tempest

On January 31, 1940, law clerk Ida M. Fuller of Ludlow, Vermont, received the first monthly Social Security check (check number 00-000-0001) in accordance with the Social Security Act of 1935. Although Ms. Fuller only paid a total of $22 in Social Security taxes throughout her years of work, she lived to be 100—and therefore collected some $20,000 in benefits.

Negation:
Crank up the respirator. Somebody owes me money.

Doublethink means the power of holding two contradictory beliefs in one's mind simultaneously, and accepting both of them.

—George Orwell, *Nineteen Eighty-Four*

If there is any danger lurking in the daily negation, it is the danger of the double negative.

By starting each day with a negation, are you inadvertently *affirming* your negativity? Does this book make you feel *happy* about your curmudgeonly disposition and cynical outlook on life? Do the rules of grammar apply to psychology? Do the rules of grammar even apply to everyday language? If two negations in one sentence equal an affirmation, why do two affirmations in a sentence equal a double affirmation? When the kid climbing out your window with a familiar VCR says to you, "I ain't stealin' nothin'!" do you really believe that he's straining for a more convoluted way to say, "I *am* a crook"? Who knows? We're just throwing this out to give you something to worry about.

Negation:
Today I'll groan about the unfairness of language and ask: Why *don't* two wrongs make a right?

A hole is nothing at all, but you can break your neck in it.

—Austin O'Malley

Groundhog Day is a day of celebration for pessimists everywhere. For one thing, it is the only national holiday built entirely upon a hole. For another, it is highlighted by an event in which a group of severely light-deprived city fathers in funny suits actually roust a potentially cranky, funky-smelling, hibernating rodent out of its lair—an animal that has been fermenting the same food in its stomach for several months!—certain that what they will get for their trouble is an early whiff of spring-time.

Meteorology has become a complex science. It is quaint to think that a fat-storing, semiconscious mammal with a brain the size of a pea is capable of predicting the weather—but hey, Willard Scott has got to work someplace.

Negation:
If ever I decide to crawl into a hole, it won't be in Punxsutawney, Pennsylvania.

Diplomacy—The art of saying "Nice doggie" till you can find a rock.

–Wynn Catlin

Christmas for Christians (or anyone who needs new handkerchiefs) is December 25. Orthodox Christmas is January 6. But if you want to give a thoughtful tchotchke to a mass-murdering tyrant, the accepted date for that gesture is February 3.

Czechoslovakia, the fruitcake of Eastern Europe, was passed to Hitler in 1938. Seven years later, it had been reduced to a few sticky crumbs. Nevertheless, at the Yalta conference, which began on this date in 1945, Churchill and Roosevelt presented its ruins and those of a few other countries ("We can't give him just Czechoslovakia. How tacky would *that* look?") to Stalin.

Negation:

If someone offers me a few hectares of smoldering Bosnian bottomland and an oil-burning Yugo, I'm in no position to turn them down.

And you take the model that what a waste it is to lose one's mind, or not have a mind as being very wasteful. How true that is.

> —Dan Quayle in a speech to the United Negro College Fund ("A Mind Is a Terrible Thing to Waste")

How *very* true. Being born on this date in 1947 put Dan Quayle right in the demographic middle of the sex, drugs, and rock 'n' roll generation. Since he has neither sex nor drugs nor the influence of Ozzy Osbourne to blame for the wasted condition of his mind, it is a matter of some curiosity how he came to be such a curiosity.

Sex? He isn't up for it. ("Anyone who knows Dan Quayle knows he'd rather play golf."—Marilyn Quayle.) As for chemical stimulants, it's been reported that he was in the proximity of LSD once but he didn't inhale. And everybody knows his idea of rock 'n' roll is Pat Boone—a compulsion that might inspire to insulin dependence, but no illicit pharmaceutical intake.

Negation:

Why do I have to work so hard for the vapidity Dan was handed on a silver platter?

The most serious charge which can be brought against New England is not Puritanism but February.

—Joseph Wood Krutch, *The Twelve Seasons*

You simply haven't lived until you've endured a quaintly interminable New England winter. There is a fire roaring in the hearth, bringing the room temperature up to a level suitable for penguin-breeding. The ruddy-faced children are passing the lung-shredding cough they developed in October back and forth like a pestilential hacky-sack. And just when you think things couldn't be worse, a neighbor comes by with some venison jerky—about the time that friendly little fawn you've been feeding stops coming by at all.

Negation:

I will invest in a Currier & Ives print when I find one that includes a 1968 Chevy pickup stuck in a filthy snowbank or men with icicles coming out of their noses scrounging for frozen roadkill.

Well . . . ?

—Ronald Reagan

Not really, but thanks for asking.

Ronald Reagan, who made our day by revealing that his doctors had found him "sound as a dollar," was born on this date in 1911.

Negation:
Have a jelly bean. You'll feel better.

Every compulsion is put upon writers to become safe, polite, obedient, and sterile. In protest, I declined election to the National Institute of Arts and Letters some years ago, and now I must decline the Pulitzer Prize.

—Sinclair Lewis, 1926

Throughout his lifetime, self-degrandizing author Sinclair Lewis, born on this date in 1885, declined many honors, including the Pulitzer Prize, the People's Choice "Most Accessible Leftist" Award, and the Grammy for Hip-hop/Gospel Crossover Newcomer of the Year. He did, however, accept the Nobel, the only prize that comes with a sizable check attached.

—— *Negation:* ——
I would graciously accept the booby prize at the American Psychiatric Association potluck antidepressant cook-off.

I don't mean to speak ill of the dead, but he was a prick—
pardon my French. He was selfish and petulant, and believed his own press releases.

—Rock Hudson on James Dean

The only drawback to being an angry young man is
that it often prevents you from becoming an angry old
man.

James Dean believed himself to be a force against the
unyielding societal mores of the fifties. On September 30,
1955, his small speeding Porsche became a splatter
against the equally unyielding American sedan of Donald
Turnupseed.

The rebel without a pulse was born on February 8,
1931.

Negation:

To prove that I am a rebel, I will rip the tags off both my pillow *and*
my mattress.

Time: That which man is always trying to kill, but which ends in killing him.

–Herbert Spencer, *Definitions*

War Time, later Daylight Saving Time, was established in the United States when the clocks were moved forward an hour on this date in 1942. Since then, we've been robotically synchronizing our clocks twice a year, congratulating ourselves on "gaining" an extra hour of mind-numbing tedium or moaning about "losing" an hour we're sure would have been bliss if only it had been available to us.

The truth is that all we're really doing is making it possible to get to work on time.

Negation:
I will waste time before it wastes me.

She could have urinated on him.

> —Don King explains to Larry King (no relation) how Desiree Washington could have prevented Mike Tyson from performing oral sex on her in an Indianapolis motel room

The jury gave their verdict on this leaky piece of legal speculation when they convicted Iron Mike of rape on this date in 1992.

Negation:

He could have been boxing's man of the hour, instead he spent three years afraid to drop the soap in a state prison shower.

If you are of the opinion that the contemplation of suicide is sufficient evidence of a poetic nature, do not forget that actions speak louder than words.

–*Fran Lebowitz, Metropolitan Life*

On this date in 1963, Sylvia Plath, living alone with two young children through a cold winter in a London that did not yet believe in central heating, knelt on her kitchen floor and put her head in an unlit gas oven.

Negation:
Cooking is not necessarily therapeutic.

The ballot is stronger than the bullet.

—Abraham Lincoln, Speech, 5/19/1856

Today was Honest Abe's birthday before it was combined with Washington's on the third Monday in February. The quote here just goes to prove that an honest opinion does not necessarily equal truth. Nor does it even ensure you an uneventful evening with your shopaholic and probably manic-depressive wife at the theater.

Negation:

I need a ballot proof, I mean bullet proof, vest.

Men think they're more important than women because
their suit jackets have secret pockets on the inside.

–Rita Rudner, *Rita Rudner's Guide to Men*

The delusion of importance under which men operate
has less to do with secret pockets than with a lack of
oxygen supply to their "brains." For the secret to male
success lies not in the hidden places they keep their
wallets, little black books, and other proofs of virility,
but in the necktie.

More than just a *symbol* of enslavement to the corporation, the silk noose performs a vital function. A
mental shackle tied stylishly in place acts as a tourniquet
to restrict the flow of oxygen-bearing red cells to the
gray matter. A man is then free to concentrate on the
deadening rote of spreadsheets and organizational charts
without the annoying interruption of "thoughts," "feelings," and other evidence of cerebral vitality.

Negation:
Clothes make the man miserable, but manageable.

One special form of contact, which consists of mutual approximation of the mucous membranes of the lips in a kiss, has received a sexual value among the civilized nations, though the parts of the body do not belong to the sexual apparatus and merely form the entrance to the digestive tract.

—Sigmund Freud, *The Sexual Aberrations*

A kiss is still a kiss. Happy St. Valentine's Day.

Negation:
Two words: Mucous membranes.

Failure is impossible.

–Susan B. Anthony

As any optimist will be only too glad to point out: Nothing is impossible.

Suffragette Susan B. Anthony was born on this date in Adams, Massachusetts, in 1820.

Negation: ─────
In my own small way, I will strive to do the possible.

Politicians are one step below used-car salesmen. So Sonny's perfectly at home there.
> —Cher, on the election of her first ex-husband to Congress in the Republican landslide of 1994

Apparently nothing much has changed in the down-again, down-again relationship between the tattooed one-woman circus, Cher, and her diminutive former ethnic sideshow. Still, as Marianne Williamson's bankbook will attest, this is the "new age" of enlightenment and personal transformation. And in this exciting "new" age, nobody—not even Traci Lords—exemplifies the boundless human potential for self-reinvention like Salvatore "Sonny" Bono.

Born on this date in 1940, Sonny Bono was lucky enough to find a love that *did* pay the rent, and quite nicely, too. But when his monomial mate ousted him from her bed, her life, and his role as her prime-time spittoon, Congressman Salvatore "Sonny" Bono (R., Palm Springs) pulled himself up by his elevator boot straps. With minimal assistance from a blissfully forgetful public, he miraculously transformed himself from a pop star with a bad haircut and fuzzy mukluks in arguably the tackiest milieu on the West Coast into a politician with a bad haircut and tasseled loafers in arguably the tackiest milieu on *any* coast.

Negation:
The beat go on.

Population, when unchecked, increases in a geometrical ratio. Subsistence only increases in an arithmetical ratio.
–Thomas Robert Malthus, *The Principle of Population*

Thomas Robert Malthus was born on February 17, 1766. We're willing to bet that he didn't look back on his own birth as part of the population problem that made him famous and added the word Malthusian to our bloated vocabularies.

— *Negation:* —
I am not the exception to the rule.

It's not the most intellectual job in the world, but I do have to know the letters.

—Vanna White

As Laurence J. Peter so amblyopicly put it, "Competence, like truth, beauty, and contact lenses, is in the eye of the beholder."

Happy Birthday, Vanna. We hope you realize how lucky you really are. We don't know a single four-year-old who, given a stepladder to reach the top row and a good reason to grin like an idiot, couldn't be doing your job.

Negation:
I'd like to buy a "why."

Whether the earth or the sun revolves around the other
is a matter of profound indifference.
— Albert Camus, *The Myth of Sisyphus*

Well, it's a matter of profound indifference to *us*. We
feel insignificant enough without being reminded that we
are just two faceless ciphers among billions of faceless
ciphers stuck on an unspectacular planet that's buzzing
a medium-sized star in a ho-hum galaxy somewhere
within an infinite universe. But interplanetary move-
ments were not insignificant to Galileo. He had to recant
his theories just to avoid being burned at the stake. And
Nikolaj Kopernik, born in Toruń, Poland, on this day in
1473, would have been toast, too, if he had not been
indifferent to self-promotion.

Today we celebrate the book Kopernik wrote under his
rather obvious *nom de plume*, Copernicus, and the good
sense he showed in delaying its publication until after
his death by natural causes. The Copernican Revolution—
and the Match-lite briquets—could start without him.

Negation:
Discretion is the vital part of survival.

We live, breathe, and eat kids.
> —David Freilicher, Senior Vice President of "Grey 18 and Under," a unit of Grey Advertising dedicated to the marketing of children's products

Questions of cannibalism aside, the question remains: How many television commercials does it take before a child's natural *inquisition (why, why, why)* becomes a lifelong obsession with *acquisition (buy, buy, buy)?* David Freilicher, and every glassy-eyed parent who has ever trod the aisles of Toys 'R' Us, knows.

Oh, sure—you can try to protect your offspring from a premature descent into materialism by banning everything but PBS from your house. But even then they'll start whining for a die-cast model of the Frugal Gourmet, a truckload of Victory Garden compost, a Bill Moyers action figure (batteries not included) that grapples with the difficult issue of faith, a garage full of power tools that would make Norm Abrams drool, and John Mc-Laughlin locution lessons.

Negation:
They whine, therefore we buy.

The sky is darkening like a stain;
Something is going to fall like rain,
   And it won't be flowers.

       —W. H. Auden, *The Witnesses*

Nor is it likely to be pennies from heaven, good day sunshine, the bluebird of happiness, or even that stockbroker who lost your life savings on that hot tip last year.

W. H. Auden, who wisely went nowhere without an umbrella, was born on this date in 1907.

Negation:

In my futile search for a silver lining, I will not lose sight of the clouds.

He was ignorant of the commonest accomplishments of youth. He could not even lie.

—Mark Twain, on the inadequacy of George Washington

The famous legend of little pyorrhea-stricken George, his trusty ax, and the cherry tree that would one day be whittled into a set of dentures that could give Mister Ed a case of TMJ, is, of course, a lie. Consequently, it was destined to become *the* object lesson on the importance of telling the truth.

Was George Washington truly incapable of telling a lie? If so, he was clearly unsuited for marriage, parenthood ("The doggies are just fighting, dear"), friendship with anyone who has ever tried on a bathing suit, membership in any church, and certainly the presidency. And if he *could* lie but chose not to? Then he would have been remembered as the founder of mime rather than the father of our country.

$\mathcal{N}$egation:

Because I can, I will tell a lie.

Always to be right, always to trample forward, and never to doubt, are not these the great qualities with which dullness takes the lead in the world?

—William Makepeace Thackeray, *Vanity Fair*

You can't get far as a poet or an artist without a creative idea. Then again, as a poet or artist, you can't get far.

But before we forget the question that George Washington left us with yesterday—whether or not our first president had the basic intellectual capability to invent a fiction—consider today's quotation. George Bush, Donald Trump, and anyone called "Muffy" provide living proof that a lack of imagination and originality has *always* been a great asset in politics, business, and society.

Negation:
The One Rule of Highly Effective People: Don't Think.

Love lasteth as long as the money endureth.

—William Caxton

On February 24, 1922, Henri Désiré Landru, better known as "Bluebeard," was executed at Versailles for murdering ten of his thirteen wealthy "fiancées" and incinerating their bodies piecemeal in his stove.

During his trial, Bluebeard confessed that he had 250 women with money to burn lined up for the same fate. He also treated courtroom observers to an unexpectedly intimate and inspirational thought on the ineffable secret of lasting love. In a statement that cut straight to the heart of one of life's most compelling mysteries, he said, "Win a woman, get her money, bump her off."

Negation:

Love lasteth as long as the money endureth, but marriage lasteth as long as you endureth.

You have gold and I want gold; where is it?
> —Henry IV to merchants at a Great Council in 1407

This affable solicitation was delivered by a fifteenth-century monarch who would gladly take a head in lieu of cash. It only goes to show you that the powerful have always felt entitled to their subjects' assets—and their subjects have always felt entitled to hide them.

Our federal income tax, which is solicited by a bureau that can only take your house, put you in jail, and hound your heirs—became law on February 25, 1913.

Negation:

I have nothing to hide.

All singers have this fault: if asked to sing among friends
they are never so inclined; if unasked, they never leave off.
— *Horace, Satires*

There has been considerable speculation (okay, make
that *some* speculation) about "the day the music died."
We humbly submit that the music actually died on February 26, 1940, in a Philadelphia rooming house not
known for its choir.

Joseph Gallagher, age sixty, was a man possessed by
much happiness—and, apparently, by the haunting
strains of the "Beer Barrel Polka." Although his fellow
lodgers disagreed on some of the incidentals (like what
had actually happened to Gallagher and at whose hand),
this much of the story was consistent: The victim had
spent the day of his death engaged in something of a
one-man Polkabration. By all accounts, Gallagher had
sung the popular ditty over and over again, at the top
of his voice, for seven consecutive hours.

In the wee hours, the serenade ceased abruptly and a
night clerk rushed to Gallagher's room. But he was a
hop-step too late. Joseph Gallagher was bleeding profusely from a slit jugular vein. He had "rolled out the
barrel" one time too many.

We can only imagine what the crime scene might have
looked like if Gallagher had had an accordion.

Negation:
Welcome to Hell. Here's your accordion. (Gary Larson, *The Far Side*)

Where does discontent start? You are warm enough, but you shiver. You are fed, yet hunger gnaws you. You have been loved, but your yearning wanders in new fields. And to prod all these there's time, the Bastard Time.

—John Steinbeck, *Sweet Thursday*

John Steinbeck was born in Salinas, California, on this date in 1902. His discontent began with his eviction from the warm womb and entry into the cold world. Just as it begins for all mice and men.

Negation:
Where does discontent end?

Richard Gere and Cindy Crawford. . . . His body's by
Nautilus and her mind's by Mattel.

                                                —Sam Kinison

The first Barbie doll was introduced by Mattel founders
Ruth and Eliot Handler at the New York Toy Fair in
February 1959.

Hailed as the embodiment of "every little girl's dream
of the future," Barbie was generously provided with
everything a vacuum with nipples needed for happiness:
a shiny Corvette, a dream house without a kitchen, a
boyfriend without genitalia, and a cerebral cortex that
made a soothing sucking noise under pressure.

Negation:

If you laid all the "Barbie dolls" that have been manufactured by *People*
magazine end to end, we wouldn't be the least bit surprised.

On seventy-five percent of calendars, this date is obsolete. If this day happens to be your birthday, then three out of every four years your birthday does not exist. If February 29 is your anniversary, you are not due your next compulsory "romantic evening" or even an overpriced dinner until the year 2000. In fact, we're not even sure you're married.

What are we getting at? It's bad enough trying to come up with 365 of these things and meet a contracted deadline. If you think we're going to dig up a quotation for a tacked-on 366th just to make up for time lost by somebody else you've got another think coming.

Negation:

If you were born on February 29, don't think it's cute to coyly suggest, "I'm about to celebrate my tenth birthday" when you're really pushing forty. People will wonder whether you've been through a thresher.

As to marriage or celibacy, let a man take which course he will, he will be sure to repent.

—Socrates

On March 1, 1809, mateless-in-Monticello U.S. president Thomas Jefferson slipped the unnervingly titled Non-Intercourse Act through Congress with only two days left in his term. Although we're a little stiff on the particulars (how could anything called the Non-Intercourse Act possibly arouse our curiosity?), the legislation apparently did little to discourage Jefferson's pointed interest in his slaves.

— Negation: —

Although the Non-Intercourse Act was repealed by James Madison on April 16, 1809, my spouse still seems to support it.

Time is a storm in which we are all lost.

—William Carlos Williams

Time is a magazine in which fatuousness is inevitably found.

It was published for the first time by Briton Haden and Henry R. Luce on this day in 1923.

— Negation: —
Time is on my hands and Life is in the crapper.

Well, you know, that's a very hard song to sing. Even opera singers have trouble with it. Whatever you do, you gotta pitch yourself low on that sucker.

—Johnny Carson's advice to Roseanne Arnold on singing the national anthem

"The Star-Spangled Banner" was designated by Act of Congress and approved by Herbert Hoover as the national anthem on this date in 1931. Hardly a toe-tapper, an ominous presence at every losing ballgame, "The Star-Spangled Banner" is the rousing combination of Francis Scott Key's paean to battle fatigue and a musical bridge that is audible only to dogs.

Featuring notes that are only reachable by grabbing your crotch and spitting, the national anthem is virtually unsingable, even by Roseanne Arnold, who has made a lucrative career, if not a life, by "pitching herself low."

Negation:
Oh, say, can you sing?

Look here, Steward. If this is coffee, I want tea; but if this is tea, then I wish for coffee.

–*Punch* magazine, 1902

At an 1896 state dinner given by Queen Victoria in honor of a visiting rajah from India, the guests are startled to see the rajah lift up his finger bowl and drink from it. When Queen Victoria picks up her bowl and drinks from it, too, the abashed guests swallow their pride and follow her lead.

It is unknown whether the queen ever saw the royal Corgis drink from the toilet.

Negation:

When sipping from the vessel of propriety, I'll be careful not to get hit with the lid.

I don't want to end up like Freddie Prinze's manager.
  —John Belushi's manager, Bernie Brillstein, March 3, 1982

John Belushi died of a cocaine/heroin overdose two days after his manager confessed this nagging fear. In addition to himself, Belushi inadvertently killed off a number of movie projects that would have made Brillstein the preeminent land shark among land sharks. He also left behind a ravenous mob of talent-eating Paramount executives; a host of parasitic Teamsters, grips, and best boys; and a snootful of toot suppliers.

Negation:
I can take them with me.

A self-made man may prefer a self-made name.

–Judge Learned Hand

On this date in 1995, vicarious kneecapper and self-made inmate Jeff Gilooley petitioned the courts to legally change his name to Jeff Stone. Although Gilooley requested the name change in order to protect his privacy (like nobody would be able to tell he was Tonya Harding's significant other by the sequins between his teeth) the case was blown into prominence when an irate group of Jeff Stones stormed the courtroom demanding that the name not be sullied.

The judge might have taken the opposition seriously had the rebellion not been led by former child-actor and sitcom-personality-disorder sufferer Paul Petersen. Petersen, who seemed genuinely confused as to whether his name was Jeff Stone or whether he had merely played a character named Jeff Stone on *The Donna Reed Show*, made an impassioned plea for justice, saying, "Have we lost our capacity for outrage? Of course I'm upset. He's ruined his name. Why should he get a chance to ruin ours?"

The judge ruled in Gilooley's favor.

Negation:

I will change my name to Beaver Cleaver just to see who shows up in court.

If you had a mobile phone, you'd be at work right now.
    —Billboard for Bell Atlantic Mobile, 1994

When did naked threats join sex ("this Camaro IROC Z is a babe magnet") and paranoia ("they hate you because you stink") in the advertisers' armamentarium? We can only hope that if Alexander Graham Bell had known the tyranny his invention would lead to, he would not have patented the first telephone on this date in 1876.

Negation:
Don't Answer.

A generation ago . . . hordes of white people fled the challenging, interracial atmosphere of the cities and settled in
the whites-only suburbs. Little did we know that a lifestyle
devoted to lawn maintenance and shrub pruning would,
in no time at all, engender the thick-witted peasant men-
tality now so common among our people.

—Barbara Ehrenreich, *The Worst Years of Our Lives*

As long as it doesn't engender any undesirable fanta-
sies of landownership in our gardeners. . . .

The Russian Revolution began on this date in 1917.

Negation:
Load up the minivan. We're fleeing to the multiplex at the minimall.

I personally think that we developed language because of our deep need to complain.

—Lily Tomlin

A person's first speech, which is a baby's cry, calls attention to the fact that conditions are no longer ideal.

—Andrei Codrescu, *Raised by Puppets*

We're alive. Prozac has been approved by the F.D.A. And all we have to do to collect long-term disability benefits is sustain a near-paralyzing back injury. What could there possibly be to complain about?

The fact that people don't come with easy-to-read expiration dates. Cody Gifford. Fulfilling your dreams and feeling your life is without purpose. Not fulfilling your dreams and feeling your life is without purpose. The current craze for strange vegetables. Undergoing past-life regression only to discover that you are the only person who has never been Cleopatra, Julius Caesar, or even Xavier Cugat. Burt Reynolds' embalmer.

Negation:
Happy Happy! Joy Joy!

Pour hot water over a sportswriter and you get instant horseshit.

—Ted Williams

Swanson improved upon Ted Williams' tried-and-true recipe in 1952 when they introduced the first frozen TV dinner—block o' turkey and mashed potatoes—to a convenience-starved American public.

A boon for busy housewives and people who weren't really hungry anyway, the TV dinner enabled cooks to re-create the familiar nuances of instant horseshit without the bother of adding water.

—— *Negation:* ——
Pour hot water over me and you get instant lawsuit.

Every time a friend succeeds, I die a little.

—Gore Vidal

Sometimes I read a book with pleasure, and detest the author.

—Jonathan Swift

We are assured that a couple of dozen people who don't even know us might buy this book. With luck, they will come to detest us. But there is a highly select group of men and women who actually remember us from high school, know us from college, or worked with us at dead-end jobs. They have loathed us unconditionally for many years.

So, if you are among the Johnny-come-latelies who have only begun to resent and detest us, we say, take a number. But if you are among the chosen few who recognized our names on this cover (or, by the good graces of our generous publisher, in an advertisement), cringed, but bought the book anyway, we say, Hi! How're you doing?

Negation:
I don't want to win Lotto so I can live off of the interest. I want to win Lotto so I can live off of the resentment of my neighbors and friends.

We cannot put the face of a person on a stamp unless said person is deceased. My suggestion, therefore, is that you drop dead.

—Letter written, but never mailed, by U.S. Postmaster General
J. Edward Day, in response to a citizen who suggested that
his own likeness be immortalized on a postage stamp, 1962

The United States Postal Service suffers from a "dysfunctional organizational culture" . . . congressional investigators said today.

—*New York Times*, October 28, 1994

The U.S. Post Office was established on this date in 1789. Since then, neither rain, nor sleet, nor empty clip has stayed these couriers from their appointed rounds. Of course, the phrase "appointed rounds" takes on a whole new meaning when you consider that, in the past ten years, thirty-four postal employees have been efficiently delivered—by their fellow sorters and carriers—to that great dead letter office in the sky.

As for the compelling snippet of correspondence we quote above, don't bother looking it up in the General Accounting Office's two-year, two-hundred-page study documenting the Post Office's "dysfunction." The Postmaster General knew better than to mail it. Written in 1962, it was bound to be published in some book long before it was ever delivered. Bad news travels fast—but not by mail.

Negation:

Guns don't kill mailmen, mailmen kill mailmen.

"That corpse you planted last year in your garden,
"Has it begun to sprout? Will it bloom this year?
"Or has the sudden frost disturbed its bed?
"Oh keep the Dog far hence, that's friend to men,
"Or with his nails he'll dig it up again!"

—T. S. Eliot, *The Waste Land*

On March 13, 1980, John Wayne Gacy, a "quiet loner type" much like the inconsequential nebbish who lives next door to you, was sentenced to twenty-one consecutive life sentences and twelve consecutive death sentences for the murder of thirty-three young men and boys whose bodies were found buried under the basement of his Des Plaines, Illinois, home.

Although the date of his execution was set for June 2, 1980, pending appeals, the state's swift retribution was not carried out until May 10, 1994. John Wayne Gacy spent more years on death row than some of his victims spent on this planet.

Negation:
The waiting, unfortunately, is not the hardest part.

Doctors are just the same as lawyers; the only difference is that lawyers merely rob you, whereas doctors rob you and kill you, too.

—Anton Chekhov

The Boston Strangler confessed to killing thirteen women. In her heyday, Typhoid Mary fatally infected only three. But the list of luminaries extinguished by their doctors—and we don't mean Dr. Kevorkian—goes on and on. Queen Anne of Great Britain did not respond well to a series of treatments that included cupping, bleeding, and blistering with hot irons. Enrico Caruso felt a stab of mortality after he was "probed" with a dirty surgical instrument. Ivan the Terrible was cured of his lust for life by a doctor who treated his nonfatal case of syphilis with a fatal dose of arsenic. Louis XIV popped his cork shortly after a physician suggested that he mull his gangrenous leg in hot spiced Burgundy. Napoléon came up short after he was administered three times the recommended dose of a laxative containing mercury. Anton Chekhov, who lived long enough to supply today's quote, learned the hard whey that fermented mare's milk is not the most effective treatment for tuberculosis.

— Negation: —
They can kill me, but they can't eat me.

Et tu, Brute?

—Julius Caesar

On this date in 44 B.C., a group of disgruntled Roman senators including Brutus (rumored to be Caesar's illegitimate son) ambushed and killed populist emperor Julius Caesar. It has been widely speculated that the assassins were aided and abetted by Olive Oyl, Wimpy, and a child of unknown parentage dressed in a bag.

Negation:
I'll gladly pay you Tuesday for an imagined slight today.

When I wake up in the morning, I think of *me* first and then my wife and then my children. I'd like to meet the guy that can honestly admit he does differently.

—*Jerry Lewis*

Jerry Lewis (Josef Levitch), selfless humanitarian and a certified Genius in France, was born on March 16, 1926, in Newark, New Jersey. The world's foremost consumer of petroleum-based hair care products, Lewis is perhaps best known for his performance in "The Nutty Transgressor," a laff-'til-you-plotz comedy in which he wakes up, fails to think of his aging wife and children, and goes off in search of less timeworn replacements.

Negation:

I will think of myself first and try not to wince.

Religion . . . is the opiate of the masses.

—Karl Marx

That may be true any other day of the year, but on St. Patrick's Day, Jameson Whiskey and Guinness Stout are definitely the intoxicants of choice.

Although the Toora-Loora and shamrock-boxer-shorts crowd may find this hard to swallow, St. Patrick did *not* drive the snakes out of Ireland. The snakes left voluntarily sometime around A.D. 1100, a date that, not coincidentally, corresponds with the advent of the Tin Whistle. And in the Emerald Isle where Paddy is actually honored as a *saint*, his feast is set aside for prayer and solemn procession . . . not for the ritualistic sacrifice of thousands of livers.

To honor the unlikely notion of sainthood, a designation that would drive anyone to drink, we offer this sobering reflection:

Negation:

Even common bar skenks begin to look like God's handmaidens after twenty or thirty beers.

America is a vast conspiracy to make you happy.
                                            —John Updike, *Problems*

On March 18, 1990, the Isabella Stewart Gardner Museum of Boston was robbed of eleven paintings and drawings valued at over 300 million dollars (one Vermeer, three Rembrandts, five Degas, one Manet, and one Flinck). As conspiracies go, that one was more successful than most (though it probably wouldn't hurt to start checking out members of the Flinck fan club).

Most conspiracies—including and especially the one Updike proposes—are destined to fail. (Happy Birthday, John!)

Negation:

Now that I've gotten you all together on this grassy knoll, come on... make me happy.

The average swallow is something of a bore, and the trouble is that all swallows are average.
—Will Cuppy, *How to Tell Your Friends from the Apes*

This is the date on which the swallows—bereft of an imaginative travel agent and without the aid of a highway-jamming Airstream caravan—traditionally return to the quaintly crumbling mission at San Juan Capistrano. If you haven't done so already, now is the perfect time to phone in your annual reservation to that not-so-quaintly crumbling resort you and your family dutifully trudge back to year after year, silverfish repellent and twenty-year-old beach balls in hand, in search of some horizon-expanding, spontaneous fun.

Just because McDonald's has discovered Bulgaria, there's no reason you ever have to.

------------------------------ *Negation:* ------------------------------
Look—there's a Howard Johnson's. Want to eat some clams?

Take the life-lie away from the average man and straight away you take away his happiness.

—Henrik Ibsen, *The Wild Duck*

Take away the hope that work will make you fabulously rich instead of terminally tired, take away the promise of eternal life, the dream that your kid will become a doctor just about the time you really need one, the faith that childbirth, like love, is lovelier the second time around, the lie your postpartum stomach will look like something other than the street map of Boston, and what have you got? The purpose of this little book in a nutshell.

Henrik Ibsen was born on this day in 1828.

Negation:

As long as you take away my ex-spouse and the pooper-scooper law while you're at it, I don't really care.

I hate the filthy season. Summer makes me drowsy, Autumn makes me sing. Winter's pretty lousy, but I hate Spring. . . . Every year, back Spring comes, with nasty little birds yapping their fool heads off, and the ground all mucked up with arbutus. Year after year after year.

—Dorothy Parker, *Ethereal Mildness*

Ah, Spring—the season that makes all things young . . . except, of course, you.

The trees are budding. You've sprouted a suspicious-looking mole. Nature's creatures are mating. The neighbor's dog has developed an unnatural attachment to your leg. The happy birds are back from Florida with a song for you. Your former employer's attorney is back from federal court with a subpoena for you.

Most of all, the flowers are emerging from their long winter's sleep to greet the sun. You are emerging from your long winter's sleep to greet your allergist.

Negation:
I'll trample through some tulips today.

Beware of a man who does not talk, and a dog that does not bark.

—Jacob Cats, *Moral Emblems*

Marcel Marceau, tacitly acknowledged master of the unspeakable art of mime, was born on March 22, 1923, in the noisy season of yapping birds and girlish laughter. That may explain his love of silence, but it's still not an acceptable excuse for turning every urban street corner into the dreaded invisible box.

Negation:
Silence is leaden.

It is my intention to leave nothing to my daughter Christina or my son Christopher for reasons that are well known to them.

—*The last line of Joan Crawford's will*

Joan Crawford thought she had the last laugh until the publication of *Mommie Dearest*, a book that would have caused her to spin in her grave if not for those damned shoulder pads.

The lesson in today's birthday girl's life is obvious: if you happen to be the mutha of them all, don't disinherit your kids. What they don't get from you, they'll make up for in movie rights.

Negation:
I *will* use wire hangers.

The last one.

—Bruce Woodcock, KO'd boxer, when asked which of Tami
Mauriello's punches bothered him most

Escape-artist-cum-punching-bag Harry Houdini has not returned from "beyond the veil" to answer silly questions like the one above. But if we could ask the magician which of Joselyn Whitehead's punches bothered him most, we'd bet our straitjackets he'd say it was "The next to the last one. Or maybe the one before that..."

One day in 1926, Harry Houdini was relaxing on a sofa when he was visited by Joselyn Gordon Whitehead, an amateur boxer. Whitehead had heard Houdini's claims that he could withstand any blow to the midsection, and asked the magician if his boasts were true. When Houdini responded that they were, Whitehead delivered several violent blows to the left side of the magician's abdomen. Houdini explained that the trick worked best when he tensed his abdominal muscles first. He then invited another punch.

Two days later, the illusionist was diagnosed with a ruptured appendix and streptococcal peritonitis. A week later, he was buried—dead—in the bronze casket he usually used for his "buried alive" stunt.

Harry Houdini was born Erich Weiss on March 24, 1874.

— *Negation:* —
I cannot even withstand a blow to my ego.

Look for the Union Label.
—International Ladies Garment Workers' Union

Today is the anniversary of the 1911 Triangle Shirt Waist Company fire in New York. Blocked exits, locked doors, rotted fire hoses, and flimsy fire escapes led to the deaths of 147 sweatshop workers.

On the 36th anniversary of that famous fire (in 1947), a mine explosion in Centralia, Illinois, killed 111.

On this date in 1995, striking major league baseball players (and some who weren't so good-looking) demonstrated the perilous nature of their working conditions by signing their names thisclose to the razor-sharp edges of baseball cards.

Negation:
What does this all have to do with me? My hundred-million-dollar salary cap was made in Malaysia.

The brain is a wonderful organ; it starts working the moment you get up in the morning and does not stop until you get to the office.

—Robert Frost

Good thing, too. Whether you're a linoleum-level broom-pusher in the home office or high-level paper-pusher in the oval office, the challenge of your mindless job is that you have to be mindless to do it. No workaday drone could possibly wade through the backwash of busywork if he were bogged down by thoughts, doubts, daydreams, or measurable brain waves of any kind. And what kind of a monkey wrench would a sudden unexpected idea throw into your day? Into your career? Into your life?

Robert Frost, who worked as a teacher and a farmer while conserving his brain power for poetry, was born on this date in 1874.

Negation:
This will be my last thought for the day.

"There's nothing to be afraid of." The ultimate reassurance, and the ultimate terror.

—R. D. Laing, The Politics of Experience

When you feel that you've feared everything there is to fear, including a too-long life, a too-brief life, unappealing diseases, and the abnormal man who always looks at you funny, it is reassuring to know that you can always fear Nothing at all.

The fear of nothingness in your life may lead you to pursue lousy jobs (the fear of having nothing) and even a lousy marriage (the fear of washing, mowing, paying for, and finally getting screwed out of nothing), but it can't hold a snuffed-out candle to the fear of nothingness after you are dead. The thought of doing nothing except finally being able to grow your nails, ad infinitum, is unthinkable without the promise of some spiritual busywork, such as harp lessons or reincarnation. And the eternal expectation of receiving nothing in the mail has spawned hundreds of far-flung, postmortem forwarding addresses, including Heaven, Valhalla, Nirvana, Hades, Purgatory, and the endless calypso party, Limbo.

So if you're trying to reassure a frightened child, be more careful with your use of language. He indeed has Nothing to be afraid of. And so do you.

Negation:
There is no dial tone in the horizontal telephone booth.

The word–coining genius, as if thought plunged into a sea of words and came up dripping.

—Virginia Woolf, *An Elizabethan Play*

On this day in 1941, fearful that her allotted sea of words had run dry, Virginia Woolf filled the pockets of her coat with heavy stones, walked into the Ouse River, and forgot to come up dripping.

Negation:

On the other hand, Stephen King just fills his pockets with hot dog money and goes to a Red Sox game.

Only a fool would say a thing like that. It's just a disgrace
to an entire generation.

—Hunter S. Thompson, *Better Than Sex*

On March 29, 1992, presidential candidate Bill Clinton
admitted that he had tried marijuana while a student at
Oxford (therefore admitting to the breaking of no *U.S.*
drug laws), but that he had "never inhaled." His comment repudiated an entire generation's main form of
communal entertainment.

Later that same year, Clinton admitted that, while he
was governor, he had tried marital infidelity with a
woman who was not his first cousin (therefore breaking
the law of averages in his home state of Arkansas). When
he added, "But, Hillary, I didn't ejaculate!" he repudiated
an entire generation's second most popular form of communal entertainment.

Negation:
Let the good times roll...away.

Jodie Foster may continue to outwardly ignore me for the rest of my life, but I have . . . made her one of the most famous actresses in the world.

—John W. Hinckley, Jr.

Ronald Reagan was shot by John Hinckley, Jr., on March 30, 1981, for some obscure reasons involving Holden Caulfield and an unappreciative Jodie Foster. Just three months earlier, John Lennon had been killed by another twenty-five-year-old white male who also claimed to have been influenced by J. D. Salinger's *The Catcher in the Rye*. We thought about reading it to look for clues, but we figured it might just cause one of us to go out and pop somebody.

Negation:
Reading is not necessarily therapeutic.

Some are weather-wise, some are otherwise.

–Benjamin Franklin

Is March going out like a lion (that is, flea-bitten and half-asleep) or like a lamb (flash-frozen in New Zealand for that mmm-mmm-fresh-from-the-field taste)? Who cares? Whether it's raining or pouring, it's still a good day to consider one of the negativist's best friends, the weather. A subject that makes up almost all of our small talk with those people we'd prefer not to speak with at all, meteorology also presents us with a daily opportunity to spread gloom. It's too cold. It's too hot. It's too dry. Won't it ever stop raining? It may be sixty-three degrees by the thermometer, but with the windchill it's thirty below. The Midwest needs precipitation. The Northwest needs sunshine. Los Angeles needs a tidal wave.

Negation:
It's a nice day... unless it rains.

April 1. This is the day upon which we are reminded of
what we are on the other three hundred and sixty-four.
                                                    —Mark Twain

Since you can fool most of the people most of the
time, today's the day to take a break from negation.
Paste a smile on that sourpuss of yours. Point out the
silver lining (what's a little tarnish?) behind every cloud.
Offer your seat on the bus to a weary-looking woman.
It has gum on it, anyway. Take your assistant to lunch—
then don't ask him to fudge about it when he's filling
out your expense account. Give an unexpected gift to
the Xerox room boys. (A simple token, like a bottle of
toner in a believable shade of currency green, is always
appreciated.) When someone comments on the change,
just say:

Negation:
April Fools'

Good fences make good neighbors.

–Robert Frost, *Mending Wall*

Good fences also make for some mighty fine dining au naturel, as proven on this date in 1459 by Vlad Dracula, known familiarly as Vlad the Impaler, prince of Wallachia.

Hungry for privacy, and never short of creative landscaping ideas, Vlad Dracula swooped down to the local torture-and-disembowelment supply and loaded the pickup with thousands of long wooden stakes. That done, he directed his cowering minions to drive the stakes through nearly all of the residents of the small town of Brasov, then had them hammered into the ground in a Martha Stewart-like classic concentric circle motif.

Filled with the pride that comes of having done it oneself, the prince then sat down to a relaxed, uninterrupted dinner within the cozy confines of a picket fence made up of Saxon burghers *en brochette*.

—— *Negation:* ——

On the other hand, I can get a perfectly acceptable rot-resistant board-on-board for about $32 per eight-foot section.

I knew her before she was a virgin.

—Oscar Levant on Doris Day

Doris Day (Doris Kappelhoff before the studio gave her her sunny *nom de cinéma*) was born on this day in 1924.

Experiencing "refloweration" at a late age is not such a curious thing. A recent survey revealed that thirty percent of American couples did the wild thing only several times a year. At that rate, virtually anything is likely to grow back.

<hr>

Negation:
Que será, será.

This office-seeking is a disease. It is even catching.
—Grover Cleveland

William Henry Harrison was such a complete candidate for president even his sinuses were running. But if you sneeze, you'll miss his place in the history books. That's because William Henry Harrison died on this date in 1841, exactly one month after catching pneumonia at his own inauguration.

Negation:
Ceremonial occasions make me sick, too.

No arts; no letters; no society; and which is worst of all, continual fear and danger of violent death; and the life of man, solitary, poor, nasty, brutish, and short.

—Thomas Hobbes, *Leviathan*

Hobbes was born on this day in 1588. Over four hundred years later, he's only remembered for three words about the natural state of existence being nasty, brutish, and short, taken out of context from a very long book.

Negation:

What three words of mine will still be remembered, even if taken out of context, in the twenty-fourth century?

My dream and goal for twenty years. Mine at last . . . It all seems so simple and commonplace.

— Robert Peary's diary, 4/6/1909

Robert Edwin Peary, Matt Henson, and four Eskimos with no talent for shameless self-promotion became the first men to reach the North Pole on this date in 1909. Like most of us who attain our lifelong goals, Peary was disappointed to find his nirvana flat and cold and of bland coloration.

Negation:
What was he expecting? Santa Claus and a barber's pole?

I invite you to sit down in front of your television set when your station goes on the air and stay there without a book, magazine, newspaper, profit-and-loss sheet, or rating book to distract you—and keep your eyes glued to that set until the station signs off. I can assure you that you will observe a vast wasteland.

—FCC Commissioner Newton Minow in a speech to the National Association of Broadcasters, May 9, 1961

On this date in 1927, the President of American Telephone and Telegraph in New York successfully demonstrated television for the first time in the United States by broadcasting the vast wasteland of Herbert Hoover's Washington, D.C., office. Appropriately, Hoover was Secretary of Commerce at the time. Even at the moment of its birth, there were never any doubts about television's primary role as a sales tool.

Negation:

Today I'll consider the Information Superhypeway and the other technological marvels being proposed for my intellectual and entertainment benefit and I will wonder: Who's behind this? and What's in it for them?

I'm youth, I'm joy, I'm a little bird that has broken out of the egg.

—James M. Barrie, *Peter Pan*

What's the only thing worse than reaching your life's goal only to find it cold and barren? Never reaching your life's goal because it was a hoax and an illusion.

On this date in 1513, Peter-Pan-Syndrome sufferer and explorer Ponce de León landed in Florida in search of the Fountain of Youth. The alarming specter of taxidermy specimen and longtime Florida resident Burt Reynolds and the proliferation of wheelchair tire retreaders in the Sunshine State should be proof enough that he never found it. Still, de León did happen upon a few well-preserved widows and a decent New York-style deli in Miami Beach.

— Negation: —

I'm age. I'm discontent. I'm a little bird that's tumbled out of its nest and into the path of a retirement community shuttle bus.

I used to be snow white . . . but I drifted.

—Mae West

Televangelist Jimmy Swaggart was put into cold storage by the Assemblies of God on this date in 1988 after he admitted publicly that he had drifted into a Baton Rouge motel room and participated in lewd acts with a prostitute.

——— *Negation:* ———
I am as pure as the driven slush.

As far as I'm concerned, there won't be a Beatles reunion
as long as John Lennon remains dead.

—George Harrison

. . . unless somebody can dig up an old tape of his we
can sing along with and the money's right.

Paul McCartney announced the breakup of the century's most overexposed band on April 10, 1970. In November 1995, the "Beatles" released two new songs based
on their dead partner's tapes.

Negation:
Ringo Starr exists to remind me that life is not fair.

I'm not going to play with any nigger. I think I'll go home
and paint my house.

—Fred "Dixie" Walker, Brooklyn Dodgers outfielder
whose nickname speaks for itself

On this date in 1947, Jackie Robinson integrated major
league baseball when he played for the Brooklyn Dodgers
in an exhibition game against the Yankees. Almost immediately, several of his melanin-deficient teammates in-
itiated a season-long reign of terror during which
Robinson was subjected daily to a barrage of verbal as-
saults, attempted spikings, and suspicious beanballs.

When Jackie Robinson was named Most Valuable
Player two years later, Fred Walker's carefully white-
washed career began to peel.

Negation:
I will not paint my house on principle. I will use an extension ladder.

His sense of humor is horseshit and I feel sorry for him.
                    —Bryant Gumbel on his ex-NBC coworker David Letterman

While we don't exactly agree with Bryant, here are
our:

Top Five Reasons We'd Like to
Hate David Letterman

5. He has a staff of well-paid writers and a view of a
   New York City strip joint; we have an obsolete com-
   puter stuck in the corner of the basement and a
   view of the furnace.
4. He owns cars that are still capable of exceeding the
   speed limit.
3. He has the opportunity to insult celebrities to their
   faces.
2. He is stalked by a woman who will actually break
   into his house and clean it.
1. Fourteen million a year.

On the other hand, he was born on this date in 1947
and we weren't.

Negation:

Dave's gap-toothed smile has made him a fixture on late night TV. My gap-
toothed smile has made me a fixture at the periodontist's office.

Familiarity doesn't breed contempt, it *is* contempt.
                      —*Florence King, With Charity Toward None*

The telephone rings. You answer it. The caller addresses you by your first name. He seems to know where you live. He sounds genuinely happy to hear your voice. (This should be a dead giveaway.) You think it must be your friend. You have *one* left after that ugly incident with the stretch pants that the ASPCA blew all out of proportion. But it is not your friend. It is not even one of the casual acquaintances who call now and then to report on the status of a recent gonorrhea test. It is a complete stranger who wants to sell you windows to replace the windows you already have.

Familiarity *is* contempt. It is contempt for your privacy. For your right to be left alone. And for your right to choose your familiars (among consenting bipeds, of course).

Negation:
"Do I *know* you?"

I cannot imagine any condition which could cause this ship to flounder. I cannot conceive of any vital disaster happening to this vessel. Modern shipbuilding has gone beyond that.

–E. J. Smith, Captain of the *Titanic*

In other words, who needs lifeboats when you've got a double-hull and the exhilarating feeling of immortality that great wealth brings?

The next time you feel sheltered from life's ups and downs by your stock portfolios, IRAs, and bankbooks, remember that late on this night in 1912, 1,500 rich and glamorous people (even little children lost their lives!) got that sinking feeling when the *Titanic* hit an iceberg in the North Atlantic.

Negation:
Just because it's liquid, that doesn't mean it's an asset.

In this world, nothing is certain but death and taxes.
—Benjamin Franklin

Inopem me copia fecit. [Plenty has made me poor.]
—Ovid

The avoidance of taxes is the only pursuit that still carries any reward.
—John Maynard Keynes

For those of you who do not believe in such gobble-dygook, psychometry is the psychic ability to divine messages from cheap costume jewelry, turtleneck dickies, toupees, and other inanimate objects. So what has this got to do with you, unbeliever? On April 15, a psychically charged date, even the most faithless among us can actually hear money talk.

The technique is simple. Open your prosperity chakra (otherwise known as your checkbook) and write your check to the IRS. Now hold it in your hand, control your sobbing, and listen. What is your hard-earned cash saying? It is saying good-bye.

----- Negation: -----
Today I'll pay the IRS without complaint, knowing that those making more than me are paying almost as much tax as I am.

I've got the farts again. I got 'em again, Charlie. I don't know what the hell gives 'em to me.
>   –Astronaut John Young to colleague Charles Duke, from the
>   official NASA transcript of the voyage of Apollo 16

On this date in 1972, Apollo 16, manned by astronauts John Young, Charles Duke, and Thomas Mattingly, strained its O-rings, achieved full thrust, and successfully blasted itself into orbit around the moon.

On April 20, Young descended to the moon's surface for a three-day rock-collecting expedition—probably by unanimous vote.

─────────────── *Negation:* ───────────────
Standing behind every great man, there is...nobody.

Here I stand. I can do no other. God help me. Amen.
—Martin Luther, standing before the Diet of Worms

Martin Luther was excommunicated by the Diet of Worms on April 17, 1521. Although we can offer no penetrating research to back this up, there is considerable evidence that the scatologically stifled schismatic may have taken the "diet of worms" thing literally. Chronically constipated, addicted to tobacco enemas (he describes the treatment in his diaries as an act in which "reverence finds its culmination"), Martin Luther may have stood before his accusers simply because he was physically incapable of sitting.

Negation:
An imploding rectum can be an even more powerful motivator than a strong conscience.

I love Paul Revere whether he rode or not.
—Warren Harding, 1923

We're pleased to report that Paul Revere *did* ride, though not long enough to develop any saddle sores.

A bit of historical background. Civil servants haven't changed much in two hundred years. Then, as now, a selfless patriot who was willing to travel the four-legged red-eye and intellectually capable of memorizing a complicated "one if by land, two if by sea" thing didn't come cheap. And neither did Paul Revere. Although he never made it to Concord, his destination, he did get on his horse long enough to start the meter running. Shortly after his mythical gallop, he billed the state of Massachusetts ten pounds four shillings for expenses incurred on a ride he never completed.

As for Henry Wadsworth Longfellow's commemorative ode about the famous nonevent that never took place on this night in 1775, that, too, may have been a payback. In 1779, Longfellow's grandfather tried to court-martial Revere for "unsoldierly behavior tending towards cowardice." Since Revere was cleared of the charges, the poem may simply have been Henry Wadsworth's way of expiating some familial guilt.

Negation:
One if by land, and two if by sea, and I on the statehouse dole shall be.

On the whole, I'd rather be in Philadelphia.
–W. C. Fields's proposed epitaph

On this date in 1956, Grace Kelly one-upped the unaccountably snobby mainline Wasps of Philadelphia by marrying the unaccountably desirable Prince Rainier III, reigning monarch of a trick question on high-school geography exams.

Although this uncommonerly lucrative career move catapulted Grace out of the cheese-steak belt, the rocky cliffs of Monaco were no place for a happy landing. The Prince had promised his bride the Sun, the Stars, and the World. They turned out to be the smarmy tabloids that squeezed the Rainiers in whenever the Kennedys stumbled onto the straight and narrow. And although Grace gamely fulfilled her part of the bargain, providing Monaco with free publicity and a balding, allegedly bilingual heir, she also got two debauched daughters in the deal that made South Street streetwalkers look like something out of *High Society*.

Negation:
On the whole, I'd rather be alive.

My mother groan'd, my father wept,
Into the dangerous world I leapt;
Helpless, naked, piping loud,
Like a fiend hid in a cloud.

— William Blake, *Infant Sorrow*

Today's a day of apprehension in Germany since neo-Nazis have become brash enough to start commemorating Hitler's birthdate. Which leads us to think about babies.

Baby Hitler, Baby Stalin, Attila the Baby, Idi Amin Baba, Little Leona Helmsley . . . they met the height requirement for cooing, oozing infancy once. They also met the blankness requirement which allowed their parents to project upon them a complete set of improbable dreams. What future careers did their parents envision when their offspring took their first steps? Did Baby Hitler goose-step across the floor? What importance did they glean from their first words? Did Little Leona kvetch, "You call this diaper clean? I wouldn't stoop to poop in this thing." Was Idi Amin a biter? Or were the hints more subtle? Even absent?

Negation:

Today I will remember that infants represent infinite potential and possibility . . . and that at least half of those possibilities are negative.

Just say the report of my death has been grossly exaggerated.

–Mark Twain, 1897

On April 21, 1910, Mark Twain died, only thirteen years after an overly zealous media reported him dead.

Negation:
Any report of any death eventually becomes true.

Hooters? What are hooters? I've never heard that expression.

> —Barbara Walters, to TV star Brett Butler during the taping
> of a *Barbara Walters Special*

On April 22, 1976, Barbara Walters became the first anchorwoman of a network television news program and the highest paid journalist in history when she accepted a five-year, $5,000,000 contract with ABC. The only journalist who found it necessary to quip, "I didn't get ahead by sleeping with people. Girls, take heart!" it can be assumed that Walters has also never heard the terms bazookas, yabos, gazongas, neh-nehs, headlights, knockers, whoopee cushions, jugs, cans, Grand Tetons . . . or wetirement.

Negation:
Ta-tas? What are ta-tas?

As an aficionado of literature it might interest you to know that in all of Shakespeare, the word *assertive* appears not a single time.

—Fran Lebowitz, *Metropolitan Life*

In the bard's defense, he scribbled his little comedies and tragedies without benefit of the thousands of enlightening, empowering self-help books for which we have felled the world's forests—and certainly without the apt assistance of the hundreds of interchangeable "relationship experts" irresponsibly bred by Ricki Lake, Montel, Geraldo, and Jenny Jones. If Shakespeare were writing today, he would have had to have mentioned that Hamlet was the disassociated product of a dysfunctional blended family; that Lady Macbeth rubbed people the wrong way, not with her overarching ambition, but with her cracked, dry, compulsively overwashed hands; that Lear was a patriarchal, withholding control-freak with dubious parenting skills; and that the Fool was, in the professional lexicon, a few fries short of a Happy Meal.

William Shakespeare (an obviously disturbed man who preferred fictional encounters and imaginary dramas to fully realized interpersonal relationships) was born on or around this date in 1564 and shed his mortal coil on this date in 1616.

— *Negation:* —
Get me to a nunnery...unless there's still room in Sex Addicts Anonymous.

I think that every time electronic equipment fails around me it is because I am feeling distorted and out of alignment.

—Shirley MacLaine, *Going Within*

Oh, and did I mention that I'm also personally responsible for the Greenhouse Effect, Talking Barbie's antifeminist diatribes ("I'd rather be a leggy dancer than Neurosurgeon Tiffany. Wouldn't *you*?"), and the 1965 blackout that short-circuited electrolysis treatments from Maine to Pennsylvania?

Apparently there's nothing like a little magical thinking to help you forget that your starlet days are long gone. Happy Birthday anyway to Shirley MacLaine, who began her latest incarnation as little Shirley MacLean Beatty on this day in 1934.

There's nothing funnier than the human animal.

—Walt Disney

On this date in 1995, The Walt Disney Company announced its plan to enter the overcrowded playpen of pediatric advice by publishing a two-volume guide to the care and feeding of its own captive audience: children. Though details are sketchy on the upcoming "Disney Encyclopedia of Baby and Child Care," the book would be incomplete without Donald Duck's unintelligible advice on speech impediments, Mickey Mouse's counsel on the importance of properly fitted shoes, Jessica Rabbit's liberal views on discipline and bondage, and Cruelle de Vil's tips for making the most out of the family pet.

─────── *Negation:* ───────
Who are these people to give me advice? Ninety percent of all Disney characters are orphans.

Russia—a riddle wrapped in a mystery inside an enigma.
—Winston Churchill

On this date in 1986, the gruel-colored sprawl then known as the Soviet Union became a riddle wrapped in a mystery inside a large radioactive cloud when a series of operator errors caused the Chernobyl nuclear reactor to burn and belch massive levels of fallout over the Ukraine and a large part of Europe. To add insult to DNA-frying injury, the famed Ukrainian nauga herds were decimated as a result of the blast, resulting in a crippling shortage of shoes, tacky upholstery, and skin-graft materials.

In 1979, a similar accident occurred near Harrisburg, Pennsylvania, when the Three Mile Island nuclear power plant, cleverly staffed with people who did not know what to do in case of malfunction, malfunctioned. Although the problem was quickly contained, the mishap spawned many eerie and inexplicable effects, including the eruption of Mount St. Helens, the election of the surprisingly lifelike Ronald Reagan to the presidency, and, most freakish, the emergence of a Philadelphia baseball team good enough to win the 1980 World Series.

Negation:
Accidents will happen...to me.

Nathan Leopold walked out of Stateville Prison Thursday into the wonderful world of free men. He promptly got sick.

—John Justin Smith, in a Chicago *Daily News* story that detailed the release of Leopold, 1958

Confinement can be hazardous, but not as hazardous as freedom.

On this date in 1865, the Mississippi side-wheeler *Sultana*, crammed beyond its 376-person capacity with 2,400 cheerful Union soldiers recently released from Confederate prison camps, burned to the waterline eight miles out of Memphis, Tennessee. At least 1,547 lives were lost in the worst maritime disaster in U.S. history.

— *Negation:* —

Jail's not so bad. You get enough bread to keep you alive and an amount of water you don't have to tread.

I ain't got no quarrel with them Vietcong. They never called me "nigger."

—Muhammad Ali

On this date in 1967, Muhammad Ali who, when the money was right, was able to manufacture quarrels with Sonny Liston, Floyd Patterson, Ernie Terrell, and George Foreman, refused to be inducted into the Army on religious and moral grounds.

Negation:
I ain't got no quarrel with the Selective Service. They never called me a yellow-bellied draft dodger. Well...maybe they did.

. . . Think how mysterious and often unaccountable it is—that lottery of life which gives to this man the purple and fine linen and sends to the other rags for garments and dogs for comforters.

—William Makepeace Thackeray, *Vanity Fair*

In 1988, William (Bud) Post of Oil City, Pennsylvania, won $16.2 million in the Pennsylvania lottery. Shortly thereafter, his brother hired a hit man to kill Bud and his wife so he could collect the winnings. Before his last lottery check ran out, Maryland's first instant millionaire, Paul McNabb, lost his job, suffered numerous break-ins, and received kidnap threats on his children. He now drives a cab in Las Vegas. When twenty-five-year-old Theresa Brunning hit the lottery jackpot in 1985, she threw a big party to celebrate. None of the invited guests speak to her now.

— *Negation:* —

As if this day hasn't been bad enough, I just found out I won the lottery.

Resolve then, that on this very ground, with small flags waving and tinny blasts on tiny trumpets, we shall meet the enemy, and not only may he be ours, he may be us.

–Walt Kelly, *The Pogo Papers* (1953)

We have met the enemy and he is us.

–Walt Kelly, *Pogo* (1971)

Between these quotes in the future and present tenses, we experienced Vietnam, the 1960s, and a good deal of confusion about who our enemies—besides Richard Nixon, the Bee Gees, and Twiggy—really were.

On April 30, 1975, helicopters lifted the last remaining Americans out of the embassy compound in Saigon. Since the end of the longest war in American history is not celebrated with any holidays, we'll mark it with a negation in the past tense.

— *Negation:* —
We met the enemy, he was us, and we both lost.

Under capitalism man exploits man; under socialism the reverse is true.

–Polish Proverb

Until very recently, this was May Day, the formerly international celebration of distress.

On May 1, 1990, Mikhail Gorbachev made the customary "No-I'm-not-secretly-dead" appearance on the balcony in Red Square. He was immediately confronted by an unruly mob of shouting, jeering comrades. Certain that the dissidents were protesting Gorbachev's reforms, the police made many arrests. Really they were just trying to let him know about the embarrassing borscht stain on his head.

─── *Negation:* ───
That's nothing compared to what happened to the 10 million people who discreetly pointed out that Stalin had spinach between his teeth.

> It's not that I'm afraid to die. I just don't want to be there when it happens.
>
> —Woody Allen

Prior to the advent of modern embalming, there was a widespread fear of waking up dead: that is, being buried alive. Those fears were not unfounded. Coma, stupor, and chronic fatigue syndrome were often mistaken for the real thing, and an alarming number of people found themselves eating dirt with only a few lily stems to pick their teeth with.

Because of these unpleasantries, The Society for the Prevention of Premature Burial popularized the "Make Sure I'm Dead" clause, a will addendum that required each corpse be "tested" to separate those who were resting in peace from those who were just resting. In some cases, the testator asked that a finger or toe be amputated prior to interment, certain that his screams would alert an ambitious undertaker to his viability.

When better-dead-than-red icommieclast Joe McCarthy died on this date in 1957, nobody checked for a "Make Sure I'm Dead" clause. They just amputated him from the body politic and added him to the permanent blacklist.

Negation:

If I'm engaging in subversive activities, I'm alive. If I'm engaging in subterranean inactivity, I'm dead.

It is far safer to be feared than loved.
—Niccolò Machiavelli, *The Prince*

Birmingham, Alabama, police commissioner Eugene "Bull" Connor celebrated Machiavelli's 494th birthday on this day in 1963 by calling out the dogs and turning the fire hoses on civil rights marchers, creating the most indelible video of that struggle and proving that he was a real "prince of a guy."

Negation:

Whatever my shortcomings, I will content myself in the knowledge that I am not a hoser.

If a little knowledge is dangerous, where is the man who has so much as to be out of danger?
— Thomas Henry Huxley, *On Elementary Instruction in Physiology*

Hint: He is not at the controls of the gravity-defying ride you're in line for at the amusement park. He is not behind the wheel of that oncoming Roto-Rooter truck. And he is certainly not in the United States Senate.

Thomas Henry Huxley born (1825).

Negation:
I am in danger.

> Hegel says somewhere that all great events and personalities in world history reappear in one fashion or another. He forgot to add: the first time as tragedy, the second as farce.
>
> —Karl Marx, *The Eighteenth Brumaire of Louis Napoléon*

A beardless baby named Karl Marx was born on May 5, 1818. Although he thought of himself as a done deal, his followers saw fit to recast him again and again, first as a guru, then as a utopian prophet of equally divided portions of manna and gruel, a philosophy, a dogma, and finally, into hundreds of glowering concrete statues. In his own lifetime this progression had already reached the point where he felt the need to tell Engels: "All I know is that I'm not a Marxist."

— *Negation:* —
All I know is that I have no followers.

In the depths of my heart I can't help being convinced
that my dear fellow men, with a few exceptions, are
worthless.

—Sigmund Freud

Sigmund Freud, who placed sex at the center of every
subconscious motivation and women on the bottom of
every sexual transaction, was evicted from his mother's
womb on this date in 1856.

Worthless though his fellow men may have been, Freud
still believed that males were an average of six inches
less worthless (eight if you're lucky) than their envious
female counterparts.

Of course, most modern therapists are enlightened
enough to know that what women really want is a cigar.
But since all therapy remains indebted to Freud's big
bang theory, and since the majority of patients in therapy are still female, it's obvious who gets the trimmed-
off end of the stick.

───── Negation: ─────
Therapy is not necessarily therapeutic.

If ignorance is bliss, why aren't there more happy people?
                                        –*Farmers Almanac,* 1966

Ignorance is bliss—but only if you happen to be a movie producer.

Forrest Gump was released on videotape in May of 1995 in accordance with the humane deinstitutionalization policies that have filled our park benches with babbling loonies who are happy to share their philosophy of life—but not their seats.

Negation:
Life is *not* a box of chocolates.

Misconceptions

We were trying to get pregnant, but I forgot one of us
had to have a penis.

—Roseanne, on her petered-out marriage to Tom Arnold

We know, Roseanne . . . little things slip your mind. But
more-or-less manly Tom Arnold might not have gotten
the shaft if somebody had thought to consult Johnny-on-
the-spot fertility specialist Cecil Jacobsen.

Known for the odd selection of magazines in his office,
a good all-purpose fertilizer, Dr. Jacobsen made a practice of spouting off on his accomplishments—until several of his unsuspecting patients discovered that he had
inseminated them with his own sperm. He was convicted
of fraud and perjury on December 28, 1992, and sentenced to five years unsolitary confinement.

Negation:
It isn't what's between my legs that makes me a man . . . then again, maybe
it is.

Every time a child says, "I don't believe in fairies," there
is a little fairy somewhere that falls down dead.
                                      —James M. Barrie, *Peter Pan*

Tempting, isn't it? (I *don't* believe in Kathie Lee Gifford.
I *don't* believe in Barney. I *don't* believe in that IRS
auditor who called yesterday. I *don't* believe in . . .)
James Barrie was born on May 9, 1860.

Negation:
It must work. I had two wisdom teeth pulled, but all I got under my
pillow was a bill for $600.

I love New York City. I've got a gun.

—Charles Barkley

On May 10, 1849, huffy members of the hoi polloi and just about every other blight on Broadway topped off a night of depraved thespianism by engaging in something even uglier than the traditional post-theater prix-fixe dinner: the Astor Place Riots.

Uppity British actor William Charles Macready had already affronted sophisticated New Yorkers with his comments on the vulgarity of American culture. But when he insisted that the ill-bred, tastelessly clothed theater-going crowd adhere to a strict dress code during his performance of *Macbeth* at the Astor Place Opera House, he incited the city to an even higher than normal level of pique. Anxious to disprove the vulgarity charge, a wild-eyed mob debated Macready with clubs. Then they used paving stones to shatter the windows of the theater during his performance. Order and quiet were not returned to the streets of lower Manhattan until troops opened fire on the crowd, killing twenty-two and wounding fifty-six.

Negation:
I want to spay and neuter *CATS!*

All Dalí's most beautiful paintings are of Gala. I wonder what he would have painted if he hadn't married her. And his watch hadn't melted.

—Andy Warhol, *Exposures*

And we wonder what Andy would have painted if he hadn't stumbled into the soup aisle at the local A&P. And Marilyn Monroe hadn't self-destructed.

Salvador Felipe Jacinto Dalí i Domenech was born on this date in 1904.

Negation:
If art really imitated life there would be more paintings of cigarette butts, frozen lasagna, and toilet paper.

. . . Of making many books *there is* no end; and much study *is* a weariness of the flesh.

—*Ecclesiastes* 12:12

Floods, plagues, pestilence, disobedient women who are abruptly turned into salt licks . . . what made the authors of the Bible so darned grumpy? Simple. Not only did biblical collaborators work centuries before the advent of the word processor, they ghostwrote the bestselling book of all time with no hope of ever collecting so much as a drachma in royalties.

--- *Negation:* ---
I won't even write a postcard unless I see some cash up front (*or* I am working before the advent of the invention that will make me obsolete).

More than at any time in history mankind faces a cross-roads. One path leads to despair and utter hopelessness, the other to total extinction. Let us pray that we have the wisdom to choose correctly.

—Woody Allen

Fab, Biz, Wisk, Tide, All, Bold, Cheer . . . the choices are dizzying. But they all lead to the same end—hours of drudgery punctuated by moments of regret about the lemon-fresh panacea not taken.

Accountant, movie star, rocket scientist, driveway repair scam artist, surrogate mother . . . the choices are dizzying. But they all lead to the same end—hours of drudgery punctuated by moments of regret about the other roads to drudgery not taken.

Negation:
I'll take the other one.

There's a richness to sadness that's missing from happiness. Anybody can be happy.

—David Byrne

The richness that comes from sadness cannot be deposited in the bank—but it can deposit you in a vault.

The head Talking Head was born in Dumbarton, Scotland, on this date in 1952.

Negation:
I am rich in ways my accountant will never understand.

The grass is always greener on the other side.
— *Early advertising slogan for lawn fertilizer*

And so are the shrubs, and the trees, and the money. Author L. Frank Baum, who knew that the Emerald City limits did not begin "somewhere over the rainbow" but just beyond the property line, was born on this date in 1856.

— Negation: —
There's no place like somebody else's home.

A racetrack is a place where windows clean people.

—Danny Thomas

The first Kentucky Derby was run at Churchill Downs, Kentucky, on this date in 1875. The immortal winner was Aristedes, with a time of 2:37 and 1/4. The losers' names are lost to history, but their mortal remains are still holding together some rather fine antiques.

Negation: ————

Winners come in first. Losers come in glue pots.

I'm all for Lawrence Welk. Lawrence Welk is a wonderful man. He used to be, or was, or—wherever he is now, bless him.

—George Bush, squirming verbally after attacking a Lawrence Welk museum as government pork during the 1992 New Hampshire primary

Wherever he was, or used to be, on the day of this curious comment, Lawrence Welk did not two-step off the edge of the land of the living until May 17, 1992, exactly three months *after* the New Hampshire primary.

George can be excused his confusion; after all, Lawrence Welk was eighty-nine. The opalescent bubble of his television popularity had long since burst. In other words, he had already joined that great crowd of fading celebrities whose vital status is known only to a handful of anxious heirs, an aging group of hard-core fans, and active participants in annual celebrity death pools. Current members of this group who could be living, dead, or at some awkward stage in between include: Red Skelton, Mitch Miller, Abe Vigoda, Mason Reese, Ken "Eddie Haskell" Osmond, Burl Ives, Jim Backus, Al Lewis, Minnie Pearl, any professional sports star who retired more than twenty years ago, and any rock musician who appeared at the original Woodstock.

— **Negation:** —
Look alive.

Term, holidays, term, holidays, till we leave school, and
then work, work, work till we die.

-C. S. Lewis, *Surprised by Joy*

On May 18, 1852, Massachusetts passed the first statute
making school attendance mandatory for all Bay State
eight- to fourteen-year-olds. (Yes, even the Kennedys.)
    Having been eager-eyed adolescents ourselves, we un-
derstand that C. S. Lewis' inspirational quote may seem
a little harsh to those potential dropouts who are still
in school, looking forward to life in the "real world."
Still, it is an improvement over the alternate scenario:
Jail, parole, jail, parole, then jail, jail, jail till you die.

-------- Negation: --------
Any spring break experienced by an adult comes with a plaster of paris
cast.

You don't know anything about a woman until you meet
her in court.

—Norman Mailer

Henry VIII, who had already learned enough about the
problems of severing the bonds of matrimony after his
run-ins with Catherine of Aragon and the Vatican,
avoided any further knowledge of his second wife, Anne
Boleyn, by having her beheaded on this date in 1536.

In the sixteenth century, nonsurgical alternatives to
marital discord were complicated novelties. To axe for
a divorce, on the other hand, was accepted practice.
Besides, Henry was an old hand at executions. Anne
Boleyn and Catherine Howard would have been just a
couple of temporary faces in the crowd of Henry's 72,000
other victims if not for the titles that put them head and
shoulders above the rest.

Negation:
Hey, the vows don't read, "'til *natural* death us do part."

I should like one of these days to be so well known, so popular, so celebrated, so famous, that it would permit me . . . to break wind in society, and society would think it a most natural thing.

—Honoré de Balzac

Human exhaust is 100% natural, to be sure. It is organic. It contains no artificial colors. (Too bad, too; a discreet tint would make those pesky anonymous emissions much easier to trace.) But just because an end product is natural that doesn't make it down-home good.

Radon is natural. So are phlegm, dirt, aging, maggots, guests of the *Ricki Lake Show*, cow pies, tooth decay, anything that comes out of a baby, fungus, slugs, and Gloria Steinem's hair color.

Honoré de Balzac—who has reached a spreadable consistency but will never be found on *our* fat-free crisp bread—was born on this day in 1799.

Negation:
It doesn't matter whether I shop or not. I still figure prominently in America's gross natural product.

If you're so smart, let's see you get out of the Army.
> —Casey Stengel, in reply to a fan in uniform who criticized his managing

On Armed Forces Day, when hundreds of crisply uniformed men and women parade their unfailing courage, unabashed patriotism, and, if you're lucky, a couple of jeeps down the streets of American towns both large and small, you cannot help but brush a tear from your eye and recall that most stirring of poetic anthems:

> "Breathes there a man with soul so dead,
> who never to himself hath said,
> 'At least I can always claim to be gay.'"

Negation:
I am 4-F: fat, flat-footed, four-eyed, and demonstrably female.

He looked at me like he had just smelled a pile of dead fish. Like I was a leper, or something awful. He'd say something like, "Oh how simply ravishing, my dear." But he really wanted to throw up.

—Marilyn Monroe on meeting Sir Laurence Olivier

Laurence Olivier, classically trained ichthyologist who could sniff out a glassy-eyed, bloated-gilled fluke past its prime from forty paces, was born on this date in 1907.

Negation: ———
Really, I want to throw up.

Sic transit gloria mundi. [Thus passes the glory of the world.]

On this date in 1876, Joe Borden of Boston pitched the first no-hitter in professional baseball history. In spite of earning that permanent and lofty place in the annals of athletic trivia, he ended the season as the team's groundskeeper.

—— Negation: ——
Shit happens. To prove it, and to honor the spirit of Joe Borden, I will spread manure over my lawn.

We are not amused.

—Queen Victoria

Queen Victoria, grammatical gang-of-one, whose unique idea of pluralism extended only to herself and any other preternormal protoplasmic ooze that managed to walk, crawl, or leach out of her lucrative gene pool, was born on this day in 1819.

Negation:
Neither am we.

Philanthropy is the refuge of rich people who want to annoy their fellow creatures.

—Oscar Wilde

In a 1986 event called Hands Across America, nearly 6,000,000 people who could not come up with a plausible previous engagement linked hands to form a human chain that stretched 4,150 miles (with breaks for deserts, popular bars, and other geographical landmarks) from New York City to Long Beach, California. The mass interdigitation, which sponsors hoped would raise $50,000,000 to aid the homeless and hungry, engendered numerous traffic jams, a rash of broken acrylic nail tips, an annoying resurgence of uplifting folk songs, and the all-round good feeling you just don't get from philanthropic gestures that aren't broadcast on all three major networks.

Negation:
Charity begins at home. So I stayed there.

What good can it do an ass to be called a lion?
                                    —Thomas Fuller, *Gnomologia*

The naming of children is a serious matter, though you would never know it from the number of girls born in the eighties who were named after the blond heroine of *Dynasty* or New York's most famous jewelry store.

Although the naming of boys tends to be a less imaginative pursuit, there is an alarming tendency among new parents to evoke the macho "They're-a-gunnin'-for-ye-Kidd" patina of the Old West by calling their horse-deficient sons Cody, Jake, Jeb, Wyatt, and every other saddle-sore variant short of Hoss, Hardtack, and Trigger. Before you are tempted, on John Wayne's birthday, to add to the list of names that make our kids' kindergarten rosters sound more like the casualty list from the OK Corral, consider that faux cowboy John Wayne's real name was Marion—you know, like the maid. And that the most notorious of his namesakes are John Wayne Gacy and John Wayne Bobbit.

Negation:
OK, I'll call him what my parents called me—"Stoppit."

The costumes of women should be suited to her wants and necessities . . . while it should not fail to conduce to her personal adornment, it should make that end of secondary importance.

—*Amelia Bloomer*

Amelia Bloomer, born on this date in 1818, was a feminist, temperance leader, influential social commentator, and the founder of *Lily*, the first newspaper published by and for women. Not quite 180 years later, she is remembered only for advocating a change in women's underwear.

— *Negation:* —

In a hundred years, all Gandhi will be remembered for is a droopy diaper.

The victim does not suffer at all. He is conscious of nothing more than a slight chill on the neck.

—Joseph Ignace Guillotin

The guillotine was built by a French surgeon, Dr. Antoine Louis, with the help of a German harpsichord builder, Tobias Schmidt. When the lives of Louis XVI and Marie Antoinette were found to be in need of a trim, the machine that took a little off the top was still correctly known as the "Louisette."

Enter Joseph Guillotin (born 1738), well-intentioned buttinski and soon-to-be-infamous do-gooder. A minor politician who believed that if you're going to kill somebody you might as well be nice about it, Guillotin was instrumental in pushing a law through the French National Assembly that required capital punishment to be carried out humanely by "means of a machine." The next thing he knew, one of the most barbaric means of execution was named after him.

Apparently, the general public felt the "guillotine" had a nice metallic ring to it. Despite Guillotin's protests, his name remained forever connected to the device. After his death in 1814, the family spent years in court trying to sever all ties to the machine their ancestor did not invent.

Negation:
I'm an advocate of rectal thermometers, but I'm sure as heck going to keep my mouth shut about it.

The strangest whim has seized me . . . After all I think I
will not hang myself to-day.

                              –G. K. Chesterton, *A Ballade of Suicide*

And in all probability, you won't, either. Although
spring is the most popular season for self-inflicting all
manner of mortal wounds (and Martha Stewart suggests
we spend it mulching!), hanging is the method of choice
among *teenagers*. In other words, if you have lived long
enough to make a will, withdraw from friends and relatives, experience sudden and extreme changes in
weight, suffer from insomnia, feel worthless or "unnecessary," exhibit apathy on the job, behave irrationally,
use alcohol, or display any of the other myriad warning
signs of impending suicide, chances are you're off the
hook.

G. K. Chesterton was born on this date in 1874.

Negation:
The strangest whim has seized me...After all I think I will not harangue
myself today.

On the day of the race, a lot of people want you to sign something just before you get in the car so that they can say they got your last autograph.

—A. J. Foyt

Gentlemen, go to your tombs. The first annual Indianapolis 500 auto race and deathwatch was held on this date in 1911. The winner, Russ Harroun, completed the 500-mile course in 6 hours, 42 minutes, and 8 seconds at an average speed of 74.5 miles per hour.

The Indy 500 is held, appropriately, on Memorial Day.

Negation:

No matter how fast I go, I always spend most of my time in the pits.

> As flies to wanton boys, are we to the gods;
> They kill us for their sport.
>
> —William Shakespeare, *King Lear*

Two thousand, two hundred people who had cleverly situated their homes at the bottom of a gorge and at the junction of two rivers (Riv-vus. Bring snorkel. Must see!) were killed when the 450-acre Lake Conemaugh drained itself into the area surrounding Johnstown, Pennsylvania.

The flood that dampened spirits and washed out the long holiday weekend of 1889 was considered by many to be an "act of God." It was actually the act of a group of Pittsburgh industrialists who were richer than God. Recognizing that a large body of water was *the* essential accessory to a pair of L. L. Bean waders, they purchased the man-made lake as their own private fishing preserve. With no thought to such details as the buildup of water pressure, or the problem of finding good help underwater, they removed the discharge pipes to keep the water level even, then blocked the spillways so their fish could not escape.

—— *Negation:* ——
Who died and made you God? Andrew Carnegie? Okay, just checking.

If at first you don't succeed,
Try, try again.

—William Edward Hickson, *Try and Try Again*

The history of the second most famous cliché of perseverance, *Don't give up the ship!*, is appropriate today. It was uttered by Captain James Lawrence on June 1, 1813, as he lay dying on the deck of the *Chesapeake* during a naval engagement off the coast of Massachusetts in the War of 1812. Not only did Lawrence give up the ghost, but the ship was defeated and captured by the British.

In the end, not even Lawrence's immortal battle cry survived intact. What he really said was—and we're not making this up—"Don't give up the ship. Blow her up!" He was obviously having trouble with another cliché; he thought the ship was supposed to go down with its captain.

Negation:
If at first I don't succeed, I won't beat a dead horse. I'll blow it up.

Marriage, *n.* The state or condition of a community consisting of a master, a mistress and two slaves, making in all, two.

—Ambrose Bierce, *The Devil's Dictionary*

Ah, the season of the blushing bride—and of her temporarily essential accessory, the groom. With apologies to T. S. Eliot, June may, in fact, be the cruelest month, breeding $200-a-pop invitations among the utility bills . . . mixing bridesmaids of irregular shape with dresses of irresponsible hue . . . stirring what began as momentary lust into life sentences for two without the hope of parole.

Be generous with your gifts. Marriage is an institution wherein two live more cheaply than one wants to. And divorce lawyers cost more than the happy couple thinks.

Negation:

Today I will bask in the knowledge that married couples do not really live longer than unmarried people. It just seems that way.

A guy scores a goal, runs around the stadium shaking his fists, suddenly sinks to his knees, and everybody on the team f***s him dog-style.

—Dan Jenkins

Soccer, a game of quick end runs that can take the unsuspecting flanker by surprise, made its first appearance at American colleges in 1820, not so much as a sport but as a form of hazing. Upperclassmen, who presumably understood that they were supposed to kick the ball, routinely kicked freshmen instead. At Harvard and Yale, players often passed the ball to teammates they disliked. As for the freshmen, it was in their best interest to keep the games low-scoring.

Soccer was banned during the 1830s because of the large number of injuries sustained by students. It was repopularized in the U.S. in the 1970s after the advent of modern proctology.

Negation:

I know people who play soccer. Only they skip the goal part. And the running around part.

First love is a kind of vaccination which saves a man from catching the complaint a second time.

–Honoré de Balzac

But the 2,532nd love . . . that'll get you where it hurts.

Giovanni Casanova, who "vaccinated" thousands of women, men, and slow-moving beasts in his fifty-year sexual rampage across Europe, fathered an uncountable number of illegitimate children. His famous kiss-and-tell book, written in the afterglow of his brief encounters with, among others, an Italian nun, a Russian lieutenant, and his own daughter, Leonilda, numbers 4,545 pages in length.

But Casanova got his in the end. He was treated eleven times for various venereal diseases before the age of forty and died in 1798, at age seventy-three, of complications of syphilis, gonorrhea, and chronic prostatitis.

Negation:

You can read the story of my sex life on the side of any mayonnaise jar: Best when used by August 15, 1984.

Practical men, who believe themselves to be quite exempt from any intellectual influences, are usually the slaves of some defunct economist.

–John Maynard Keynes, *The General Theory of Employment Interest and Money*

Double your prospects for intellectual slavery! Today's the birthday of not one but two defunct economists—Adam Smith (1723) and J. M. Keynes himself (1883). Between them, they filled thousands of pages with millions of impenetrable paragraphs on capitalist economic theory, so that we wouldn't have to think at all—beyond the one simple economic truth that we all understand too well:

Negation:
The bucks stop elsewhere.

A wide screen just makes a bad film twice as bad.
                                          —Samuel Goldwyn

Unless that wide screen happens to have been plunked down in the middle of the urban tundra, as was the first drive-in movie theater, which opened on this date in 1933 in Camden, New Jersey.

Although the drive-in movie screen was wide enough to encompass both George Lucas' immense vision of endless space and the vast, sucking vortex between Carrie Fisher's ears all at the same time, the drive-in proved to be a merciful antidote to bad film. Hanging a speaker on your window to hear Ryan O'Neal ease Ali MacGraw—and an entire generation's capacity for apology—into premature death was like hanging a seashell on your ear to hear the syringes wash up on a New Jersey beach. Nor, mercifully, could you see, what with the windows steamed up and all.

Drive-in movies have since gone the way of Mia Farrow's career: they set the scene for countless frightening conceptions, then disappeared. But if this reminds you that there might be someone still locked in your father's trunk, it's time to let him out.

Negation:

Because there is nowhere left to neck, I'll just skip to the good part.

I'm going to live to be one hundred, unless I'm run down
by a sugar-crazed taxi driver.

—*J. I. Rodale*

Unfortunately for the *Prevention* magazine publicity
department, he missed his prediction by about thirty
years.

On June 7, 1971, Jerome I. Rodale, septuagenarian
health-food nut and creator of the preeminent periodical
for medical establishment paranoiacs, died of a heart
attack in his chair after extolling the virtues of bonemeal
during a taping of the artery-suffocating *Dick Cavett
Show*. ABC respectfully broadcast a rerun rather than
going for the ratings coup.

Negation:
I may live until tomorrow unless I'm wrong.

I can't sing and throw up at the same time.
                    —Grace Slick on the impossible demands that prompted her
                    departure from the Jefferson Starship in 1989

On June 8, 1994, fifty-four-year-old Grace Slick revealed that she had at last mastered the complicated juggling act we call life by pleading guilty to charges that she had pointed a shotgun at police officers while simultaneously ranting, raving, and reeling about the grounds of her Tiburon, California, home.

Under a plea bargain agreement, she agreed to attend three months of Alcoholics Anonymous meetings, perform two hundred hours of community service, submit to random drug testing, and abstain from alcohol.

Negation:
I've already done my community a service. I moved out.

Every form of addiction is bad, no matter whether the narcotic be alcohol or morphine or idealism.

—Carl Gustav Jung

Every form of addiction is great for business, unless you happen to be Carl Jung. He was born too soon to become part of the great codependency economic boom. But you weren't.

If you're not an idealist yourself, you are sure to have one in your family. You need help!

Negation:
I will start confronting my addiction or codependency to idealism with the twelve-step program outlined tomorrow.

The whole world is about three drinks behind.
— Humphrey Bogart

Alcoholics Anonymous was founded on this date in 1935. Since then, four generations of hopelessly alcohol-addicted drunks have transformed themselves into hopelessly dependency-program-addicted twelve-steppers. So why is it still so difficult to find a choice bar stool at the local watering hole? Because twelve steps are simply too many for today's busy alcoholic.

But the harried addict can save brain cells as well as time by treating the Twelve Steps like the Ten Commandments and skipping over the time-wasters. Including:

Step 5. *I've admitted to myself and to another human being that I have been a fool.* You've peed into potted plants. You've become inexplicably teary over the song "My Ding-A-Ling." Where do you suppose you're going to find one other human being who wasn't previously aware that you've been a fool? Skip.

Step 10. *I have made a searching and fearless personal inventory and, when I was wrong, promptly admitted it.* It takes time to confess to every Tom, Dick, and Harry whose lamp shades you've defiled. If you must bare your soul, cut to the chase and confess to Barbara Walters. What the heck, it worked for Bill Clinton.

Negation:
Is the nearest bar more than twelve steps away?

It would seem that the universe is thirty billion light-years across and every inch of it would kill us if we went there. This is the position of the universe with regard to human life.

–Martin Amis, *The Information*

E.T. The Extra-Terrestrial, Steven Spielberg's clever recasting of Christ as a bug-eyed sprite, opened on this date in 1982.

It, along with the *Star Wars* trilogy and the infinite variations of *Star Trek* ("To boldly go where we have made money before"), exist to assure us there is something "out there" besides unbreathable atmospheres of sulfur and methane, an infinite vacuum that would pop us like a poodle in a microwave, and highly evolved species that would view us as nothing other than laboratory specimens or a refreshing break from potato chips.

Negation:
I'll boldly go as far as the mailbox. Beyond that, forget it.

We can't all be heroes because somebody has to sit on the curb and clap as they go by.

–Will Rogers

Another "role model" got kicked to the curb on this date in 1994 when the bodies of Nicole Brown Simpson and Ronald Goldman were discovered outside her L.A. condo. So go ahead and add "the Juice" to your ever-lengthening list of sullied celebrities and tainted athletes whose tarnished images dashed briefly through the bustling airport of mass-appeal (including Pete Rose, Mike Tyson, Tonya Harding, Michael Jackson, Jennifer Capriati, Dana Plato, and, alas, Pee-wee Herman) only to nose-dive into the great rent-a-Bronco counter that lies beyond.

─── Negation: ───
I will say no to the temptation to model my life after anyone else's, realizing that I have even less control over their actions than I have over my own.

Saints are all right in heaven, but they're hell on earth.
—Richard Cardinal Cushing

Your cackling aunts can accurately be described as a coven. Your reprobate cousin cannot be left alone in any bathroom that's stocked with aerosol tub and tile cleaner. You're wondering, "Why can't my family be more, you know . . . *saintly?*" They *are* saintly. That's why your life is hell on earth.

St. Martin de Porres is a case in point. He set up a cat and dog hospital . . . not at his own ascetic hovel but at *his sister's house*. ("I'm telling you, it's only for a few days. I'll deliver them from distemper, teach them the rhythm method, and *pfft*! They're outta here.")

And now that we mention it, isn't Blessed Emilina, who mortified herself by wearing a hair shirt and iron chain, a lot like the daughter who mortifies you daily with her pierced tongue and braided body hair?

To sum up, there are only two differences between your uncanonized loved ones and certified saints. Saints are dead. And saints, like St. Anthony whose feast is celebrated today, can actually be of some assistance when you've misplaced the car keys.

Negation:

Actually, the vow of perpetual chastity was *my* idea.

America it's them bad Russians
Them Russians them Russians and them Chinamen. And
them Russians

—Allen Ginsberg, *America*

It's them male ice skaters who don't play hockey. It's them ice skaters them ice skaters and them people who put rain slickers and red rubber boots on dogs. And it's them flying Elvi. It's them flying Elvi and them sex educators who believe that meaningful human contact is achievable by two people with dental dams in their mouths. It's them kids who go to any school called an "*école*." It's them kids and them Cadillac drivers who will never wear out their turn signals. It's them magazine articles called "Ten Sure Signs You've Got a Terrible Disease You Will Wish Were Fatal." It's them people who put the rotten strawberries on the bottom of the package and all the good ones on top. It's them cab drivers who won't give change for a twenty. It's Andy Rooney.

Negation: ──
On the other hand, maybe it's just me.

I don't give a damn for a man that can spell a word only one way.

—Mark Twain

While visiting a Trenton, New Jersey, school on this date in 1992, Dan Quayle proves that he can only spell a word one way—the wrong way—by adding an "e" to a student's correct spelling of potato.

Muhammad Ali to flight attendant: *Superman don't need no seat belt.*

Flight attendant: *Superman don't need no airplane, either.*

Sure, we laughed when television stations began airing a disclaimer before each *Superman* rerun. ("Warning: This program contains scenes of human flight unaided by aircraft. Do not attempt at home.") We know that kids don't have a problem differentiating the Man of Steel from the Man In a T-Shirt with Sewn-In Rubber Padding. But somebody might have clued in George Reeves.

Reeves, who made 104 appearances as TV's Defender of Truth, Justice, and the American Way, did everything he could to convince himself that he was Superman. He developed a capacity for alcohol consumption that was beyond the powers of mortal men. He padded his otherwise plotless life with a cast of shady characters, including gamblers, pill-poppers, and members of a crime syndicate. And, like his alter ego, he could only get his career off the ground when he was wearing blue tights.

Unfortunately, George Reeves was not faster than a speeding bullet. He shot himself with a .30-caliber pistol on June 16, 1959, just four days before his scheduled wedding. He left no suicide note, assuming that Clark Kent would do a nice write-up in the *Daily Planet*.

Negation:

Fortunately, I have no doubts about my mortal powerlessness.

All things dull and ugly
All creatures short and squat
All things rude and nasty
The Lord God made the lot.
★   ★   ★
Each nasty little hornet
Each beastly little squid
Who made the spikey urchin,
Who made the sharks? He did.
                    —Monty Python, *Montypythonscrapbook*

On June 17, 1963, the U.S. Supreme Court ruled 8–1 that recitation of the Lord's Prayer or Bible verses in public schools was a violation of the first amendment. We offer these verses from the book of Monty Python as an acceptable substitute and a violation of just about every amendment thereafter.

—— *Negation:* ——
Now I lay me down to sleep / while things beneath my bed do creep.

Paul McCartney . . . has become the oldest living cute
boy in the world.

—*Anna Quindlen*

Paul McCartney, the only complete set of petrified remains not under the full ownership of Michael Jackson,
was born in Liverpool on this date in 1942.

Of course, musical history proves that Paul McCartney
is much more than the oldest living cute boy. He is a
cute boy who writes cute lyrics and lives on a cute farm
where he raises sheep that are too cute to eat. In other
words, he has carved an entire life out of cute, which
is a lot like sculpting a functioning brain out of Velveeta.

To date, only a handful of celebrities have managed to
milk cute like a cash cow: They include John Davidson,
Shari Lewis, Alvin and the Chipmunks (with the obvious
exception of Simon), Sally Field, Shirley Temple, and
Benji.

Negation:

There is no such thing as a sheep that's too cute to eat. And that goes
double for the sock with the Jeri-Curl on Shari Lewis' hand.

I would rather see my four daughters shot before my eyes than have them grow up in a Communist United States. I would rather see those kids blown into Heaven than taught into Hell by the Communists.

> —Pat Boone at the Greater New York Anticommunism Rally
> at Madison Square Garden

At least it would have delivered the rest of us from the eternal torment of "You Light Up My Life."

The wholesome alternative to Syrup of Ipecac, and a .45-caliber blast as a father, Pat Boone was born in June 1934. The first Father's Day was celebrated on this date in 1910.

Negation:

Father's Day? I think I'll just shoot the afternoon with my dad.

Lizzie Borden took an axe and gave her mother forty
whacks; When she saw what she had done, she gave her
father forty-one.

—*Anonymous*

What in the world could have inspired a self-made
orphan and jump-rope ditty to fly off the handle like
that? The same things *your* kids start kvetching about
when a power outage knocks Nickelodeon out of service
and they regain their power of speech.

Number one on Lizzie's hit parade of grievances was
her mother—or more specifically her *step*mother, an un-
popular fixture in 28% of American households. Number
two was her penny-pinching father. Worth a quarter of
a million dollars when he unexpectedly cashed it in on
the living room couch, Andrew Borden could have af-
forded to strip the shelves of stereoscopes (the Sega
systems of the past) and bestow them on his daughter,
but he did not. What could Lizzie do but cut short his
life? Finally, Lizzie Borden complained of boredom—
sound familiar?—a condition that was only temporarily
alleviated by her trial.

Lizzie Borden of Fall River was found not guilty on this
date in 1893 by a jury of nine people who also had well-
meaning mothers and fathers.

— *Negation:* —

Today I'll buy my kids anything that could possibly liven up their bleak
and dull middle-class existences…as long as it doesn't require sharpening.

If I was looking for Josef Mengele, my first thought would be to check the ushers in Yankee Stadium.

–Bill James

On this date in 1985, a body discovered in—of all places!—São Paulo, Brazil, was officially identified as that of Nazi war criminal Josef Mengele.

—— Negation: ——

If I was looking for Jimmy Hoffa, my first thought would be to check the chili in Giants Stadium.

He figure resembles the giant economy-size tube of toothpaste in girls' bathrooms: squeezed intemperately at all points, it acquires a shape that defies definition by the most resourceful solid geometrician.

—John Simon on Judy Garland

Judy Garland died of "an incautious self-overdosage of sleeping pills" on June 22, 1969. Her handpicked successor, chosen from the medicine chest of unexpired celebrity, was her daughter Liza Minnelli, on whom most of the intemperate squeezing has been applied directly to the head, nose, and face.

Negation:
I can be replaced.

I don't feel we did wrong in taking this great country away from them. There were great numbers of people who needed new land, and the Indians were selfishly trying to keep it for themselves.

—Faux cowboy John Wayne

William Penn, second in popularity only to the Liberty Bell if one is to judge by the names of diners and motor lodges along the Pennsylvania Turnpike, signed his peace treaty with the Indians on June 23, 1683. We're not sure what promises the famous Quaker made to the Indians— maybe a stack of bingo cards and one of those handy little hamster cages that mixes up the numbers. All we know is that Penn ended up with everything he could see from the top of Philadelphia City Hall. And the Native Pennsylvanians got to go from being the sole possessors of a historically significant commonwealth to 0.1% of the population in the 1990 census, the lowest percentage of any state in the union.

—— Negation: ——
You can't scalp me. I'm already bald. And I can't get any decent reservations, either.

The entire evening gave me a headache for which suicide seemed the only possible relief.

    —Rex Reed reviewing *The Rocky Horror Picture Show*

Why would anyone feel bad after watching ninety-five minutes of eyeliner "don'ts" as demonstrated by a coven of kinky ghouls? Because he just paid $7.50 for something you can see for free in any middle school in America.

Negative audiences have one unmanipulable emotion: despair. And at least despair comes cheap. Our picks for the top three feel-bad classics won't be packing them in at the multiplex this week, but they can be rented for a song. We suggest you pay in advance.

3. *Scenes from a Marriage* by Ingmar Bergman. Get the full six-hour version. It will seem like forever until you realize that one day *you* might be married—and that funfest will run a lot longer than six hours.

2. *Rocky*. Dain-bramaged meat-packer becomes fabulously rich and famous, a premise that's just too much like real life to bear.

1. *It's a Wonderful Life.* About halfway through, you become convinced that Mr. Gower was the pharmacist on duty when you refilled your prescription for Zantac, and you just washed down two with a beer.

—— *Negation:* ——
Bring me a tub of that quadruple-bypass popcorn. Make my day.

> If you want a picture of the future, imagine a boot stamping on a human face—for ever.
>
> —George Orwell, *Nineteen Eighty-Four*

If you want a picture of the past, imagine dozens of writers, male, female, and gender indeterminate, named George.

George Orwell was born Eric Blair in India on June 25, 1903. So George is not his real name. Actually, we have reason to believe that "George" is never a real name. George Eliot, who did a little writing for *Masterpiece Theatre* and maybe an episode or two of *My Mother the Car* but that's unconfirmed, was a woman named Mary Ann Evans. She changed her name to that of her married lover, a trend that did not catch on, or we'd all be hearing about Donald Maples and Bill Flowers. George Sand was also a woman, born Amandine Aurore Lucie Dupin. We don't know why she chose George as a pseudonym, christened, as she was, after a perfectly acceptable bean dish. It might have been because she suffered from chronic constipation rather than the infinitely more trendy consumption and felt left out of the artsy scene. So she went with the "John Doe" of literature.

Negation:
We don't know what George Wallace and George Steinbrenner's real names are. But we know what they've been called.

He is the Pied Piper to the children of the world.

—Margrethe II, queen of Denmark, on Danny Kaye

On this date in the year 1284, the Pied Piper—who, in a shocking twist, was subsequently identified as elfin Hollywood petroglyph Danny Kaye—lured 130 children out of the town of Hamelin, Germany, and into oblivion.

Though the investigation continues, no link has been established between "the Piper" and the sudden and complete disappearances of Kaye costars Dana Andrews, Virginia Mayo, Glynis Johns, and the entire cast of the 1952 clunker, *Hans Christian Andersen*.

Negation:

Is that a flute in your pocket or are you just glad to see me?

When I was a kid I once stole a pornographic book in braille and rubbed the dirty parts.

          —Woody Allen

We all have our little blind spots, don't we? Some of us can't see the forest for the trees. Others among us can't see the difference between a pornographic book in braille and a young Asian "stepdaughter." So we can all admire (and sometimes envy) the total sensory deprivation of Helen Keller, tireless advocate of the waffle iron as literature and an example of something or other to us all, who was born on this date in 1880.

Negation:

There are none so blind as those who cannot see.

Power is the ultimate aphrodisiac.

—Henry Kissinger

Judging from the virulent good looks and congenital magnetism of Henry VIII, it must be.

Henry was about twenty-two when he acquired a skin disease characterized by multitudinous festering boils. So of course Catherine of Aragon believed him when he promised her the moon. He had come to resemble it.

In his thirties, he added chronic debilitating headaches and an unhealing leg ulceration to his repertoire. When he was forty-five, Henry VIII made Anne of Cleves the jewel in his crown. Destiny gave him a gift in kind—a red, rubbery tumor that topped off his bulbous nose like the cherry on a curdling sundae.

By the time he married Catherine Howard, Henry had reached the peak of his come-hither-and-bring-the-doctor-with-you good looks. His festering leg had reached elephantine proportions. And his eyes were buried in folds of fat. In 1543, Catherine Parr succumbed to Henry's daunting charm. Weighing in at four hundred pounds, he could no longer manage sexual intercourse—which probably did more for the cause of eroticism than the invention of the chastity belt.

Henry VIII, who, along with English sweating sickness, was the catch of his day, was born on June 28, 1491.

Negation:
Isn't Marlon Brando still available?

The only reason I'm in Hollywood is that I don't have the moral courage to refuse the money.

—Marlon Brando

On this date in 1894, the first Monday in September was designated as a national holiday: Labor Day. The idea of Labor Day was to give workers a taste of relaxation, to liberate them from columns of numbers and piles of paperwork, and free them from the stresses of jockeying for position at the fax machine. Consequently, most Americans celebrate Labor Day by bolting a taste of carcinogenic charcoal-burned chicken, joining the columns of people piled up at the amusement park gate, or jockeying for position at the forty-seven tollbooths between them and the beach.

Negation:

The only reason I'm wearing this hokey barbecue apron is that I lack the moral courage to refuse a day off.

Just do it.

—A sneaker company's slogan

Just do *what*? Become active, vital, sexy, happy, healthy, popular, skinny, and rich? That might annoy your friends, but it doesn't do the sneaker company any good.

Just do what then? Just pay a hundred and seventy-five dollars for your kids' running shoes without asking any silly questions about why two-dollar imitation PF Flyers were good enough for you.

Negation:
No one will ever kill me for my footwear.

Fat guys need idols, too.

—Mickey Lolich, 6-foot, 250-pound pitcher

By now you've realized that your fitter friends—all of whom have swimming pools—will not allow you to get through the summer without squeezing yourself into a bathing suit that looks like a bag full of squalling cats. Tell them you'd love to—then ask the hostess discreetly if she thinks chlorination is any match for that nasty bacterial flesh-eating disease.

While the rest of the party-goers fight for the ladders, you'll be free to dive into the bean dip.

Negation:
A waist is a terrible thing to mind.

My God! What is there in this place that a man should
ever want to get in it?
> —James Garfield on the siege of the White House by hordes
> of Republican office seekers

Actually, we hear that Amy Carter carved her initials
into her Pennsylvania Avenue bedroom woodwork (mercifully, she stopped short of a naturalistic self-portrait).
But that factor could not have incited "disgruntled office
seeker" and sloppy job-jacker Charles J. Guiteau to shoot
President James Garfield on this date in 1881.

When Garfield finally died seventy-nine days later, with
the help of incompetent doctors, at his beach house in
Elberon, N.J., he became the second U.S. president to
have been assassinated.

Negation:
Nobody will ever kill me to get my job.

I thought the only way anybody would leave the Stones was in a coffin.

> –Keith Richards on the Internet commenting on Bill
> Wyman's desertion of his mates in 1994

Always contrary, twenty-five-year-old Brian Jones left the Rolling Stones via his swimming pool on July 3, 1969.
Exactly two years later, twenty-seven-year-old Jim Morrison exited the Doors by way of his Paris bathtub. In between those two dates the disbanded Beatles leaped into obscurity from a London rooftop (4/10/70), Janis Joplin checked out on Big Brother from a Los Angeles hotel room (10/4/70), and Jimi Hendrix ended his brief encounter with Experience of any kind (9/18/70) from his bed.

Negation:
Getting there can be all the fun.

I wander through each chartered street
Near where the chartered Thames does flow,
And mark in every face I meet
Marks of weakness, marks of woe.

—William Blake, *London*

As Bette Midler put it, "When it's three o'clock in New York, it's still 1938 in London." On this, the Fourth of July, we consider the weary, time-warped, dysfunctional parent from whom we declared our independence on this date in 1776. If we hadn't, it would still be 1938 here, rather than the rollickingly repressive return of the McCarthy era.

Negation:

If, on this Independence Day, I see any rockets' red glare or bombs bursting in air, I will know I've wandered too close to the neighborhood Planned Parenthood clinic.

Insurance, *n.* An ingenious modern game of chance in which the player is permitted to enjoy the comfortable conviction that he is beating the man who keeps the table.

—*Ambrose Bierce, The Devil's Dictionary*

Life, health, fire, auto, flood, travel, theft, liability, disability, deposit, unemployment, and accidental death and dismemberment. Though we just paid lip service to independence yesterday, it makes us feel better to know that, should we lose an integral body part in a freak Salad Shooter™ incident, someone else will accept the financial responsibility.

Bierce is right: insurance is a gamble. But unlike the gambles made in Atlantic City and Las Vegas, these bets are not made in the hope that Lady Luck will smile on us. They are based on the more realistic notion that we will be visited by darker forces. In other words, the odds are in our favor.

Negation:
I am my own liability.

I'm just here for the drugs.
> —Nancy Reagan, deftly brushing off a political question at a
> "Just Say No" rally

Suspiciously goggle-eyed former first lady and grand old party-girl Nancy Reagan was born on this date (and though the year is in some dispute, it was a year very early in the twentieth century).

Over the years, Nancy Reagan has taken a lot of heat. It has been said that, as a mother, she was a profoundly talented actress. It has been speculated that, as a deeply emotional and complex human being, she could have been the first artificial heart donor. But through it all, Nancy Reagan has remained true to her personal *raison d'être*. She has always stood behind her dope.

Negation:
What am *I* here for?

It's a scientific fact that if you stay in California, you lose one point of IQ for every year.

—Truman Capote

On July 7, 1846, Commodore J. D. Sloat of the U.S. Navy raised the U.S. flag at Monterey after the surrender of the Mexican garrison there, and proclaimed the annexation of California. He could not have known that it would be like annexing an 800-mile-long plastic wind tunnel.

The state that temporarily defines our western coast (subject to movement of tectonic plates and Nevada's ability to get a really good agent), California is a place where the ground moves but breasts don't, where mass murderers can thrive as long as they look healthy, where junkies roller blade to the methadone clinic and every avocado is under option.

Negation:

If Pamela Anderson stays in California one more year, she'll be a potted plant.

If you look like your passport photo, you're too sick to travel.

—*Anonymous*

The first U.S. passport was issued on July 8, 1796. Unfortunately, the photo was so bad that posterity will never know to whom that historic document was issued. Still, there are members of the "jet set" who mark this anniversary, and for proof of that, you need look no further than the marks on passport office clerk Mary Polik's head.

On July 8, 1985, mattress-commercial diva Joey Heatherton allegedly forced her way to Mary Polik's payment window. Unaware that the passport office is an exact-change-only bureaucracy, Heatherton handed the clerk a one-hundred-dollar bill to pay for her $42 passport.

Unfortunately, Polik informed everybody's pal, Joey, that she could not make change. That's when the forty-something star allegedly grabbed the clerk by the hair, wrenched several handfuls from her scalp, and began to drub Polik's head against the formica counter, shrieking, "I have to go to Paris. I HAVE to GO to PARIS."

Whether Heatherton made it to Paris, we cannot say. As for Polik, she filed a $6-million lawsuit against her attacker, enough to pay for a lifetime of bad passport photos—and a really decent hairweave, too.

Negation:
If you wait on Joey Heatherton, you will be too sick to travel.

Life is a sexually transmitted disease.
                    —Guy Bellamy, *The Sinner's Congregation*

On this date in 1981, an experimental drug, acyclovir, was found to be effective against the second most widespread sexually transmitted disease: herpes simplex.

Nobody has discovered an effective treatment for the first.

————— Negation: —————
Life—the gift that keeps on giving.

The chief contribution of Protestantism to human thought is its massive proof that God is a bore.

                –H. L. Mencken, *Minority Report*

The second most important contribution of Protestantism is the massive proof that human beings were all created in His image.

John Calvin, the Protestant reformer with the name so dull it sounds like an alias, was born on this date in 1509.

                Negation:
I am damned if I am, and damned if I'm not.

The good die young—because they see it's no use living
if you've got to be good.

—John Barrymore

It isn't easy being too good to live—especially when
you aren't too young to die. That was the case of found-
ing father and stationary target Alexander Hamilton, who
turned his overactive conscience into an underactive
heartbeat on this date in 1804.

Hamilton was inspired to become a Christian at age
forty-four, shortly after his son, Philip, was killed in a
duel. His strong religious feeling did not prevent him
from calling his longtime political enemy Aaron Burr
"despicable" and "dangerous," and soon Hamilton himself was preparing for a duel.

Even so, Hamilton resolved that he would not take a
life. When the gun was placed in his hand, he insisted
that he would only fire into the air. He never got the
chance. At the command, Burr fired, hitting Hamilton in
the abdomen. Still, he remained the font of goodness.
As he fell, Hamilton cautioned his second to be careful
with the gun lest it "go off and do harm."

Alexander Hamilton died for his principles at age forty-
seven. He left a good example, a financially strapped
wife and seven children, and a good-sized divot in the
grass.

Negation:

Stand up for your principles and you'll end up lying down.

The rarest quality in an epitaph is truth.

—Henry David Thoreau

Henry David Thoreau was born on this date in 1817. The hero of the young middle-class communards of the 1960s, he had much in common with the trust-fund anarchists who found him so appealing.

In the sixties, young disestablishmentarians declared themselves free from their attachment to money, but they always knew there was somebody to call if the transmission went on the VW van. Thoreau built his famous cabin close enough to Mom's so he didn't have to be bothered with the laundry.

When Vietnam era protesters recount their harrowing experiences in jail, they skip over the part where Daddy bails them out. When Thoreau recounts in *Civil Disobedience* his decision to go to jail rather than pay taxes that would support the Mexican War, he skips over the part about his aunt paying his taxes so he only had to spend one night in the local hoosegow.

Finally, in the sixties, politically correct students burned their draft cards. On April 30, 1844, on a fishing trip near Concord, Thoreau accidentally set fire to the woods, incinerating 300 acres.

Negation:
Next I suppose you'll be telling me that John Lennon wasn't a working-class hero at all but a rich guy who lived in the Dakota....Oh.

The country will be very pleased—the country is so bowel-minded anyway . . .

—Dr. Paul Dudley White reporting on President Eisenhower's health

President Ronald Reagan underwent surgery to remove a cancerous tumor from his colon in 1985. Alexander Haig was never heard from again.

Negation:

If I had my hemorrhoids removed my address book would be completely blank.

The French are sawed-off sissies who eat snails and slugs and cheese that smells like people's feet. Utter cowards who force their own children to drink wine, they gibber like baboons even when you try to speak to them in their own wimpy language.

-P. J. O'Rourke

It is Bastille Day—the commemoration of the date the French stormed the largest jail in its largest city to let the motley rabble of street vermin, caged indigents, rot-gut-guzzling guttersnipes, petty criminals, pigeon-eaters, toilet paper counterfeiters, and all-round nasty people *out*.

And you wonder why you can't find a single *citoyen* willing to direct you to the nearest McDonald's with civility?

Negation:

I don't need to travel halfway around the world to be treated like a worthless spitwad stuck to the bottom of someone's shoe. I have children.

> For the first time in the history of our country the majority
> of our people believe that the next five years will be worse
> than the past five years.
>
> —President Jimmy Carter, July 15, 1979

The next five years are always worse than the past five years if only because we emerge from them five years older. But we didn't want to hear a president tell us the obvious truth, so we replaced him with an infernal optimist who turned what would have been five lousy years into eight.

—— *Negation:* ——

In five years I will be _____ years old.

Following a nuclear attack on the United States, the U.S. Postal Service plans to distribute Emergency Change of Address Cards.

–Federal Emergency Management Agency (FEMA), Executive Order 11490 (1969)

Every mushroom cloud has a paperwork lining.

On this date in 1945, the first atomic bomb was dropped on the unsuspecting rattlesnakes and kangaroo rats of Alamogordo, New Mexico. Exactly three weeks later, it was proven equally effective on unsuspecting humans.

Now that nuclear weapons are in the hands of third-world dictators who can't think of any constructive way to control population, it's reassuring to know that our subscriptions to Martha Stewart's *Living* ("Irradiate your own vegetables!") and encouraging messages from Ed McMahon ("Your children will have three eyes. So the prize you may have won will look three times as big!") won't get lost in the fallout.

Negation:

My checks, however, will still be "in the mail."

> What's in a name? that which we call a rose
> By any other name would smell as sweet.
>
> —William Shakespeare, *Romeo and Juliet*

On this date in 1917, the British Royal Family ethnically cleansed their blue bloodlines and valiantly aligned themselves with the winning side in World War I by changing their name from "Wettin von Saxe-Coburg und Gotha" to "Windsor" (after the castle).

Princess Elizabeth, the current queen, ran into a similar problem with the name of her fiancé, Philip Schleswig-Holstein-Sonderburg-Glucksburg. He was introduced in the press as Lt. Philip Mountbatten, although he cheerfully answers to "the cipher."

Negation:
I'll call myself the Earl of Negative Equity—after *my* castle.

The reason that there are two senators for each state is so that one can be the designated driver.

—Jay Leno

Sen. Edward Kennedy should have remembered this rule. If he had, he probably wouldn't have driven Mary Jo Kopechne and his presidential aspirations off a bridge on Chappaquiddick Island on this date in 1969.

Negation:
Shit floats.

The pursuit of the Inner Child has taken over just at the moment when Americans ought to be figuring out where their Inner Adult is, and how that disregarded oldster got buried under the rubble of pop psychology and specious short-term gratification.

—Robert Hughes, *Culture of Complaint*

Judging by the popularity of Mazda Miatas and orthodontia for adults, we know you've found your inner child. But should necessity demand it—somebody in the house has *got* to be able to use pointy scissors—how do you get in touch with your inner adult?

Five Ways to Summon Your Inner Adult

1. Owe any amount of money to the IRS.
2. Discover that a disease has been named after you . . . and you are not a doctor.
3. Attempt to balance your checkbook—and not on your nose.
4. Figure out how much it's going to cost to send your kids to college and then remember how you spent your college years.
5. Compare your age to a random sampling from today's obituaries.

Negation:

I'm not getting older; I'm getting bitter.

The qualities and capacities that are important in running—such factors as willpower, the ability to apply effort
during extreme fatigue, and the acceptance of pain—have
a radiating power that subtly influences one's life.

–Jim Fixx

And, less subtly, one's vital signs. Fifty-two-year-old
shaman to the shinsplints set and go-for-the-golden-
gates jogger Jim Fixx died on this date in 1984 while
running for no good reason.

Robbery

A man who has never gone to school may steal a freight car, but if he has a university education, he may steal the whole railroad.

—Franklin D. Roosevelt

America's first train robbery took place on this date in 1873 when one-room schoolhouse dropout Jesse James dropped in on the Rock Island Express. The heist netted him three thousand tax-free dollars.

Hold up your basic hell-on-rails Amtrak passenger car today and all you'll end up with is a half-empty can of spray cheese, a cup with somebody's teeth in it, and maybe a stray kid or two.

Negation:
I prefer the Metroliner. At least there's a possibility of nicking some Brie.

Is it progress if a cannibal uses a knife and fork?
—Stanislaw Lec, *Unkempt Thoughts*

Not anymore. You may think of Head and Shoulders as an entrée rather than a personal hygiene item. You may even consider Hackensack more a pastime than a place. But you simply cannot consider yourself a state-of-the-art homovore until you've equipped yourself with handcuffs, a sledgehammer, a power drill, a handsaw, a good pair of "heavy-duty chemical resistant gloves," a hypodermic needle, an eighty-quart kettle, and, of course, a toothbrush. How do we know what it takes to get a head as a cannibal? These were among the many distinctive kitchen gadgets discovered in Jeffrey Dahmer's larder by the Milwaukee police on this date in 1991.

Negation:

Today I will consider the plight of those who are living hand to mouth—
and hope they are not living next door.

I came to the conclusion many years ago that almost all crime is due to the repressed desire for aesthetic expression.

–Evelyn Waugh, *Decline and Fall*

By the time this book sees print, the Republican Congress will probably have gutted the National Endowment for the Arts. No, no—hold your applause. Among the recipients of this money are many imaginative performance artists who smear themselves with pudding and urinate on people and things to express, we suppose, their confusion about the location of public toilets. There is even an artist who demonstrates for those homemakers who are short on kitchen space how yams can be conveniently stored in the human rectum. How are these innovative dramatists likely to react when their aesthetic expression is repressed? How long can we expect them to "hold it"? And what about the produce? If you dropped a twenty at the greengrocer's, would you dare bend over to pick it up?

— *Negation:* —

Don't bother me. I've traded in my aesthetics for anesthetics.

One should respect public opinion insofar as it is necessary to avoid starvation and keep out of prison, but anything that goes beyond this is voluntary submission to an unnecessary tyranny.

–Bertrand Russell

In celebration of the date in 1824 when a Harrisburg, Pennsylvania, newspaper published the aren't-we-fascinating results of the first public opinion poll, we ask you: who are the 10–30% of the American poll-answering public who "don't know"? We aren't talking about individuals who, having been asked the formula for rocket fuel, simply can't come up with the precise ratio of liquid nitrogen to liquid oxygen. We are talking about people who "don't know" when asked at what end they squeeze the toothpaste tube, who "don't know" whether kids should learn about sex in school or in the more traditional gutter. People who, when asked whether a "boob job" is a slang term for a surgical technique or a summation of Vanna White's career, would fall into the "don't know" category.

If a pollster called at dinnertime (do they ever call any other time?) to ask about the identities of the don't-know cadre, we'd have to admit, we don't know. But at least we could direct them to the "moral majority." They *always* know.

─────────────── *Negation:* ───────────────
I don't know.

I would be content that we might procreate like trees, without conjunction, or that there were any way to perpetuate the World without this trivial and vulgar way of coition.

–Sir Thomas Browne, *Religio Medici* (1643)

Louise Brown, the first test-tube baby, was born in England on July 25, 1978. A fun-loving young adult imbued with what her father describes as an "inborn way with babies," Ms. Brown loves to amuse very young children by picking them up with a pipette and whirling them in a centrifuge.

Negation:
You can take the girl out of the test tube, but you can't take the test tube out of the girl.

It really bothers me that a twerp like that can parade around and convince everybody he's Satan.

—Ry Cooder on Mick Jagger

It really bothers us that Charlton Heston has convinced everybody that he's Moses, that Doris Day has convinced everybody she's a seventy-two-year-old virgin, and that the artist formerly known as Prince has convinced himself that he's a question mark with a deviated septum.

Mick Jagger, who's only managed to convince us that DNA is God's claymation, was born on July 26, 1943.

— *Negation:* —
I couldn't convince anybody that I was the Prince of Darkness if they spotted me the darkness.

All right, Edith, you go right ahead and do your thing . . .
but just remember your thing is eggs over easy and crisp
bacon.

—Archie Bunker

Although some "Dingbats," "Meatheads," and quite a
few "Polaks" thought it was a weekly telethon for big-
otry, popular consensus was that *All In The Family* raised
the consciousness of a nation by depicting us as the
opinionated, self-centered, chair-hogging, sexist, racist
but loveable people we really are. Indeed, the sitcom
was such a national phenomenon that every Saturday
night for eight years, women all over the country set
aside their frying pans, joined the family in the living
room, laughed for a full half hour, then went back into
the kitchen and finished the dishes.

Norman Lear, who put the words into Archie Bunker's
mouth (and you thought it was your father/husband/
Jackie Mason/Jesse Jackson/Andy Rooney), was born on
this date in 1922.

Negation:

I can bring home the bacon, fry it up in a pan, and raise your
cholesterol so high your doctor will think he's reading the Dow Jones
Averages.

How can we lure people away from the dreaded VCRs, whose sole reason for popularity is that most of us don't have the nerve to masturbate in movie theaters?
—John Waters, *Crackpot*

On July 28, 1991, Pee-wee Herman was arrested for "saluting the Surgeon General" (thank you, Joycelyn Elders!) in an adult movie theater in Sarasota, Florida.

If the summer of '69 was the summer of love, then July of '91 was the solstice of sick. On the 19th, Mike Tyson was accused of raping a beauty contestant. On the 22nd, Jeffrey Dahmer was eating up the airtime. William Kennedy Smith's invasive techniques had come into question and he was awaiting trial. In comparison, Pee-wee's indiscretion seemed like a drop in the bucket. Still, the funniest man ever to grace Saturday morning television was ordered to get a grip on himself. The court sentenced him to seventy-five hours of community service and the production of an antidrug video. We, the holier-than-him public, banished Pee-wee to an indeterminate exile from our airwaves.

Negation:
If I must play with myself, I'll do it while watching Barney.

Painting

> There is no end to sorrow.
>
> —Vincent van Gogh's last words, 7/29/1890

Yes, there is. But when the sorrow does end you'll be unconscious and you won't care. So it doesn't pay to rush it along.

On July 27, 1890, after completing seventy paintings in the previous seventy days, Vincent van Gogh walked into a field outside Auvers, France, that would look familiar to any art lover and shot himself in the chest. When he discovered (*hélas!*) that he was still alive, he walked back to town and reported his embarrassing condition to Dr. Paul Gachet (a man as immortal as the "Mona Lisa" because van Gogh's portrait of him sold at auction for a record price of eighty-two-and-a-half million dollars in May 1990).

"I missed myself," Vincent complained.

His friends, the three people to whom he didn't owe money, didn't get to miss him until two days later, when he finally died, at the age of thirty-seven.

Negation:
Painting is not necessarily therapeutic.

Consumption

> Conspicuous consumption of valuable goods is a means of reputability to the gentleman of leisure.
> —Thorstein Veblen, *The Theory of the Leisure Class*

In the nineteenth century, conspicuous consumption was a noble thing. It benefitted literary heroines by providing them with countless curtain calls before the conspicuously undramatic finale. And it benefitted the world by putting an entire genre of books—those witheringly melodramatic tales hocked up by consumption-prone gentlemen of leisure—out of its misery.

Today, consumption is no less conspicuous and no less a disease. Unfortunately, the twentieth-century strain of affluenza is unlikely to prove fatal unless one is inadvertently smothered in excessive cappuccino foam.

Negation:

Today, if I'm not feeling bad, I'll go out and buy something I don't need and can't afford so I can feel guilty about it for months to come.

He was a self-made man who owed his lack of success to
nobody.

–Joseph Heller, *Catch-22*

Catch-22 was set over fifty years ago, a barbaric and
unenlightened time when people were still expected to
take responsibility for the utter futility of their lives.
Happily, today's self-made failure can attribute his lack
of success to any number of imaginative factors, including birth trauma, distant or smothering parents, unpaid
karmic debt, Anita Bryant, dispassionate teachers,
chronic fatigue syndrome, a world that does not reward
true brilliance, ego-eroding poverty, ego-eroding afflu-
ence, genetic predisposition to pattern baldness, the Pa-
pacy, the government, and the puppy that died when he
was seven.

Negation:

I would be a _____ today if not for _____.

If I owned Texas and Hell, I would rent out Texas and live in Hell.

–General Philip H. Sheridan

. . . the right of the people to keep and bear Arms shall not be infringed.

–Second Amendment to the Constitution of the United States

Texas is not a state of mind; it is a state of emergency. Texas is a stronghold of the National Rifle Association. It is also a place where, if you go to a restaurant and ask for the best seat in the house, you are shown to a chalked outline under a table. So it doesn't surprise us that on August 1, 1966, an enterprising gun-nut named Charles Whitman ushered in the longest and hottest month by climbing to the top of a tower at the University of Texas and shooting a few dozen innocent passersby.

Considering Luby's Cafeteria in Killeen, the grassy knoll in Dallas, and the charred spot outside of Waco, if we owned Texas and Hell, we'd sell them both and take our chances in Bosnia.

Negation:

Who am I to impugn the motives of those who are willing to eat lead rather than infringe on the constitutional right to pack iron?

Simple and faithless as a smile and shake of the hand.
                                                    —T. S. Eliot

On the advent of National Smile Week, remember that it takes only seventeen facial muscles to make a smile, but forty-three to make a frown.

Negation:

For once, I will do the more difficult thing.

There's nothing sadder than an old hipster.

—Lenny Bruce

Except maybe a dead hipster. Forty-year-old Lenny Bruce, who predicted, "I'll die young . . . but it's like kissing God," was found facedown on the floor of his bathroom with a needle in his arm on August 3, 1966.

Negation:
I'll die old...and it'll be like kissing Moms Mabley with her teeth out.

I launched the phrase "The war to end all wars"—and that was not the least of my crimes.

—*H. G. Wells*

You can't blame H. G. Wells for being wrong. As the doughboys of World War I understood it, they would fight and die so their sons wouldn't have to fight and die. They didn't know that war would become a federally subsidized, multigenerational recreation program under which the sons of World War I survivors would get to fight in World War II, and the offspring of World War II veterans would be rewarded with an all-expenses-paid, eight-year camp-out in Vietnam. (Korea was a boondoggle to placate the "notch-babies.")

In the opinion of most historians, the twentieth century began on this date in 1914, when England jumped into the expanding European war and gave their restless sons something to do that summer.

Negation:

If you see my son in uniform, you'll know he's gotten a job at Taco Bell.

You bastard . . . you cheat . . . you drunken bum . . . I
got enough on you to hang you. By the time I get through
with you you'll be as broke as when you got here. You
goddamn spic . . . you . . . you wetback!
> –*Lucille Ball*, graciously accepting Desi Arnaz's announcement that
> he couldn't live with her anymore

It isn't easy when someone you love breaks your heart,
bangs on your ego like a conga drum, takes you on a
fabulous vacation in Hollywood and won't let you meet
Charles Boyer. It's even worse when someone you love
uses your heart as the backdrop for the credits, bangs
everything in skirts like a conga drum, and takes you for
half of your fabulous fortune in a community property
state.

Lucille Ball, America's favorite redhead and Desi's favorite source of greenbacks, was born on August 5, 1911.

Negation:
Waaa-aaa-aaa-aaa-aaa.

Explaining to your wife why *she* needs a penicillin shot for *your* kidney infection.

> —Mike Hegan, first baseman, on "the toughest thing in baseball"

In 1928, baseball's most underrated "reliever," Alexander Fleming, cleaned out his refrigerator and discovered penicillin—thus curing the most persistent and least explainable marital itches of the world. Sir Alex, Nobel laureate for his service to mankind, was born on this day in 1881.

Negation:

One man's mold is another man's medicine.

Yes, these are the dog-days, Fortunatus:
  The heather lies limp and dead
On the mountain the baltering torrent
  Shrunk to a soodling thread
                    —W. H. Auden, *Under Sirius*

In superstitious times, brown dogs were sacrificed to appease Sirius, the Dog Star, bringer of the heather-killing heat of July and August. Living in more enlightened days, we can now simply turn up our air conditioners (and burn bigger holes in the ozone layer).

--- Negation: ---
Here, boy. Nice doggie.

Opportunity makes a thief.

—Francis Bacon

On August 8, 1945, two days after Hiroshima was bombed into a radioactive paste and seven days before Japan's unconditional surrender, the Soviet Union looked straight into the face of nonexistent fear and heroically declared war on Japan. For filling out all that complicated paperwork, the U.S.S.R. was rewarded with permanent possession of Sakhalin and the Kurile islands.

Negation:
Hey, it only knocks once.

Look, would you kindly inform him that it was *Paul Mc-Cartney* who wrote "Helter Skelter," not me.
—John Lennon's message to Charles Manson

On this night in 1969, Charles Manson proved the danger of reading messages—*any* messages—into the la-la-lyrics of Beatles songs. While most of America was busy playing *Abbey Road* backward trying to confirm that Paul was dead (We don't know what you heard . . . *we* heard, "Go buy a new needle. Now."), Charlie was holed up at Spahn Ranch speculating on the upcoming race war he and only he divined from the lyrics of "Helter Skelter." By the next day, Sharon Tate and six others were dead—and the police weren't listening to "The Fool on the Hill," they were looking for him.

In the grand scheme of things, Charlie Manson was just a malevolent dust bunny that blew into the lunatic fringe and stuck. Still, there are many theories about Charlie's motivations. He could have been after record producer Terry Melcher, the previous tenant at the Benedict Canyon estate, who did not recognize Manson and his family as the next ABBA. He could have been after Roman Polanski because of Polanski's less-than-flattering treatment of satanic cults in *Rosemary's Baby*. Or he could have been prompting John Lennon to give Paul McCartney credit where credit was due.

Negation:
Music is not necessarily therapeutic.

Sometimes when I look at all my children, I say to myself,
"Lillian, you should have stayed a virgin."

—*Lillian Carter*

One day, you're watching your happy children at play,
and suddenly you see them, not through the haze of
hopes or expectations or half a tab of Valium, but as
the unique and challenging individuals they really are.
And you think to yourself, Now I must warn the world.

Betty Ford, wife of fluke-president Gerald Ford, created
a stir on August 10, 1975, when she did just that in a
television interview. Not only did the First Lady report
that she suspected all four of her children had tried
marijuana and that she would not be surprised to learn
that her eighteen-year-old daughter, Susan, was having
an affair, she also congratulated the Supreme Court on
having made a "great, great decision" in legalizing abor-
tion.

Negation: ————
I love my children unconditionally... within reason.

I really think that I could freeze
My mother-in-law with the greatest of ease.
The only thing that gives me pause,
Is what will happen when she thaws.

                                                    —Cryonicist's ode

Many are cold but few are frozen. Unfortunately for Dora Kent, whose current address is two shelves up from the Jolly Green Giant and just down the aisle from Sara Lee, the number of human remains in cold storage awaiting thawing and "reanimation" is one too many.

The mother of cryonics activist Saul Kent, Dora suffered for years from arthritis and degenerative brain disease. When her death seemed imminent, her son hired Alcor Life Extension Foundation, a cryonics facility in Fullerton, California, to freeze his mother's head until the happy day it could be revived and grafted onto a conveniently brainless body. (Note to Alcor: Anna Nicole Smith's is available now.) Unfortunately, Alcor may have jumped the gun. There is a possibility that Dora Kent was not actually dead before her head was removed.

In August 1969, the first freezer specifically designed for the long-term vertical storage of "temporarily uncurable" (i.e., deceased) human beings was produced by the Minnesota Valley Engineering Company, but it works just as well for those Bacardi piña coladas in a can.

─────────── *Negation:* ───────────
Is there anything Mrs. Paul's won't bread?

Robert Southey will be read when Homer and Virgil are forgotten.

> –Richard Porson, professor of Greek, providing the
> marketing department of Southey's publishing house with a
> great blurb, c. 1805

We know who Homer is. We watch *The Simpsons* all the time. But who was Robert Southey? He was a very minor poet with a friend who gave a very major blurb. The truth is, it really doesn't matter if you've written a good book as long as you've got a good blurb. Consider Judith Krantz's best-seller *Princess Daisy*. Critic Clive James called it "a long conversation between two not very bright drunks." But the book jacket called it a "compelling blend of the wonder of once-upon-a-time and the pulse of the here-and-now," and it sold a zillion copies. Danielle Steel must be made of it to survive her reviews. Columnist Ellen Goodman said that *Message from Nam* was "without any redeeming social value, unless it can be recycled as a cardboard box." But *The New York Times* said, "Ms. Steel's fans won't be disappointed," and the book hit the best-seller lists. Her fans must be compulsive recyclers.

Robert Southey, an even less popular choice than Homer or Virgil if you're looking for a "sizzling, smoking page-burner of a read" (we suggest *Shot Through the Heart* by Mikal Gilmore), was born on this date in 1774.

Negation:
Lagowski and Mumma will be read when toilet paper is forgotten.

He was macabre. When I was a little girl he sent me a gift of a replica of my mother, Tippi Hedren, in a coffin. That was his idea of a joke. He had a sick sense of humor. After that, Mother never worked for him again.

—Melanie Griffith on Alfred Hitchcock

Unfortunately, "Mother" never really did a heck of a lot of work for anybody again. Which is why thinking (but, mercifully, unfeeling) people everywhere accept graciously whatever the boss gives us—whether it's a replica of a remarkably familiar-looking worker in the unemployment line or just a throbbing headache.

Alfred Hitchcock was born in London on this date in 1899.

Negation:

My boss once gave me a massive stress-related coronary. I sent a thank-you note.

There's a high rate of cancer among my friends. It doesn't mean anything.

–Dr. Francis Clifford, Health Commissioner of Niagara County,
New York, on the odd tendency of those families living near
the infamous Love Canal to develop meaningless illnesses

In August 1978, the state of New York acknowledged the several-times-higher-than-normal occurrence of purely anecdotal illnesses like birth defects, miscarriage, seizure diseases, cancer, liver conditions, and strange dermatological problems reported by the residents of the neighborhood adjoining the Love Canal and began evacuating the more than two hundred families from the area. Though the area was declared a national disaster by President Carter, and although symptoms of environmental poisoning were reported as early as 1958, the Hooker Chemical Company refused to assume the blame for the disaster caused by its dump site. Instead they ran an ad in the local paper insisting, "When you come right down to it, you'd be hard pressed to find any group of people who care as much about the ... well-being of Niagara Falls as the people at Hooker."

───── Negation: ─────
My friends all glow in the dark so brightly we use them as Tiki torches
at our barbecues. And the water is so full of iron that our kids pull all
the magnets off of the refrigerator. It doesn't mean anything.

When I appear in public, people expect me to neigh, grind my teeth, paw the ground, and swish my tail—none of which is easy.

—Princess Anne

But when she gets those shoes nailed on and she's fresh from the farrier, I'll be darned if she doesn't make it *look* easy.

Princess Anne was foaled on August 15, 1950.

Elvis Presley—bloated, over-the-hill, adolescent entertainer—had nothing to do with excellence, just myth.
—*Marlon Brando, 1979*

Pots (and we mean that literally) should be very careful when they call the kettle black. Compared to Marlon Brando, the King stayed remarkably trim, actually able to balance on a regulation-sized toilet seat, until he toppled from his throne on this date in 1977.

August 16 is an ominous date for overweight legends. Babe Ruth, who complained of his girth, "The worst of this is, I can no longer see my penis when I stand up," also chose this day in 1948 to lie down—thus minimizing the problem permanently.

Negation:

I am well-hung, if you count the parts that shouldn't be hanging.

> Home fer the winter with his family,
> Happy as squirrels in the ol' gum tree,
> Bein' the father he wanted to be,
> Close to his boys as the pod an' the pea.
> —Tom Blackburn, "The Ballad of Davy Crockett"

Not all of us can be exactly the kind of parent we want to be. But Disney-deodorized frontiersman Davy Crockett could. Born on a mountaintop in Tennessee on this date in 1786, Crockett grew up to be not only an accomplished drunk, but a rat who deserted the ol' gum tree, ran out on his wife, and abandoned his children.

In the words of syndicated columnist Harry Golden, "He was out on the frontier only because it was an easier place to live than at home with a growing brood. Davy had a flock of children and he left them and never bothered with any of them again. He set the cause of married life back two hundred years."

Davy Crockett, who apparently really did "set out grinnin' to follow the sun," was also a yellow-belly who hired a substitute to avoid going into battle in "the Injun war" and a congressman with one of the worst absentee records in history.

Negation:
My ability to nurture only sets family life back fifty years.

Those kids don't know anything. They're lying around in mud listening to a shitty sound system and eating day-old garbage, and they think they're having a good time. They're just being had, mister, had.

—Bill Graham on rock festivals

On this date in 1969, 300,000 to 400,000 mud-caked, chemically treated, hormonally hyped mammals were loaded up and carted away from Max Yasgur's farm near Bethel, New York. No, it wasn't slaughtering day. It was the final encore of the Woodstock Music and Art Fair.

Billed as three days of peace and love, Woodstock quickly turned itself into a squalid third world city where babies were born in ditches, food was flown in by helicopter, and the only medical advice was being dispensed by someone named Wavy Gravy.

All in all, it was better as a flashback.

Negation:

Now when I tell people I'm doing acid it means I'm on the Grapefruit Diet.

The past is only pleasant because it isn't here.

—Finley Peter Dunne

We didn't mind when Bill Clinton tried to stage a hill-billy revival of *Camelot* with himself as the JFK under-study and Gennifer Flowers cast in the dead-end role of Marilyn Monroe. It didn't bother us when he resurrected McDonald's french fries from the Elba of banished foods. But when he brought Fleetwood Mac (Fleetwood Mac! What's the matter? ABBA didn't return his calls?) back from the dead, it made us think twice about the desir-ability of reincarnation, the fearsome potential of cry-onics (you think we've got too many talking heads *now*?) and the wisdom of that whole spur-of-the-moment thing with Lazarus.

Bill Clinton, who made the past and at least one good reason for his political death come alive at his inaugural ball, was born on August 19, 1946.

Negation:

Please stop singing about tomorrow. Yesterday's gone. Yes, your day's gone.

The universe is merely a fleeting idea in God's mind—a pretty uncomfortable thought, particularly if you've just made a down payment on a house.

–Woody Allen, *Getting Even*

You have to be a fairly delusional person to sink your life's savings into real estate—first, because no vinyl-clad hovel you or we will ever own can properly be called an "estate." And also because any house is only as "real" as the "freak" typhoon.

Negation:

I don't know. The Up-Periscope model at Cresting River Run has a nice, semipermanent ring to it.

Judges lie, then lawyers lie, then clients lie.

—*Alan Dershowitz, US News and World Report, 10/25/93*

I have three rules. I never believe what the prosecutor or the police say, I never believe what the media say, and I never believe what my client says.

—*Alan Dershowitz, New York Times, 10/28/94*

Lawyers don't lie.

—*Alan Dershowitz, WOR Radio, 12/10/94*

There's no inconsistency here. As a defense attorney whose client list includes people you would not trust with a beauty pageant contestant, a hotel chain, or an insulin syringe, Alan Dershowitz's job is to convince a jury of only one thing: doubt. Although he had his problems with Leona Helmsley's jury (not everything can be "sanitized for protection"), he certainly succeeded with us.

The American Bar Association, the only lobbying group organized by professional liars for professional liars, came into being on August 21, 1878.

Negation:
You can't make a liar out of me. I can't pass the LSAT.

We need not hesitate to admit that the Sun is richly stored with inhabitants.

–Sir William Herschel, discoverer of the planet Uranus, 1781

Isn't it a kick to read these silly, two-hundred-year-old scientific predictions? I mean, here's the guy who actually discovered Uranus—no mean feat, as anybody who's ever been on the business end of a proctoscope can tell you—and he really believed that the sun could be inhabited. By whom? The Campfire Marshmallow Man? People in FDA-approved flame-retardant jammies? Richard Pryor?

Well, we're all sophisticated now and we know perfectly well that people can't live on the sun. We also know that as time goes on, the sun will *not* grow to enormous proportions and vaporize us, as previously thought. Most experts now agree it will only liquify us.

Negation:

Here comes the sun, do do do do, and I say, "Am I really worried that the PABA in sunscreens might irritate my skin? I want a tanning lotion that contains asbestos!"

What bereaved people need is a little comic relief, which is why funerals are so farcical.

—George Bernard Shaw

With the possible exception of the Ayatollah Khomeini's "I've got him!" "No, I've got him!" whoops into oblivion, there has never been a funeral quite so farcical as the 1926 necrophilibuster kicked off by the death of thirty-one-year-old screen idol Rudolph Valentino.

The star was laid out for public viewing at the Frank Campbell Funeral Chapel in New York City. On the first day, 30,000 souvenir-hunting mourners ransacked the funeral home. On the second day, a crowd of 50,000 women gathered. In their grief and abandon, they trampled pedestrians, smashed several store windows, and abandoned hundreds of their own pesky children in the streets.

Those who could not join the orgy fared even worse. A British actress swigged a lethal dose of poison. She died clutching a bouquet of love poems she had written for the star. An ambidextrous New York housewife shot herself with one hand while cradling her collection of Valentino photographs in the other. In Japan, two woebegone fans compensated for the absence of the smoldering star by leaping into a volcano.

--- Negation: ---

The most I can expect from my mourners is that they will swig a dose of liquor from my cabinet, flip coins for my valuables with one hand while throwing out my photos with the other, then leap into bed with my spouse.

For life in general, there is but one decree: Youth is a blunder; Manhood a struggle; Old Age a regret.

–Benjamin Disraeli, *Coningsby*

The ex-prime minister of Britain hit the nail on the head as far as the main stages of life, but he left out the transitional stages: Puberty—the comedogenic blend of blunder and struggle, and Menopause (male or female)—the intoxicating mixture of struggle and regret.

Negation:

I will celebrate the stage I'm in now, secure in the knowledge that the next will be worse.

Destiny will betray you, crush your ideals, deliver you into the same detestable Bürgerlichkeit as your father, sucking at his pipe on Sunday strolls after church past the row houses by the river—dress you in the gray uniform of another family man, and without a whimper you will serve out your time, fly from pain to duty, from joy to work, from commitment to neutrality. Destiny does all this to you.

—Thomas Pynchon, Gravity's Rainbow

Wow! And you thought you were just maturing.

— Negation: —
Maybe keeping in touch with my Inner Child isn't such a bad idea after all.

People call me a feminist whenever I express sentiments
that differentiate me from a doormat or a prostitute.
—Rebecca West

Women won the right to vote in national elections on
this day in 1920. In 1970, the fiftieth anniversary of wom-
en's suffrage in the United States was celebrated by a
march down Fifth Avenue led by Gloria Steinem, Bella
Abzug, and Betty Friedan, culminating in the historic bra-
burning. En route, the women were called many names,
none of them sounding even vaguely like "feminist."

— Negation: —
As Hillary Clinton said to Mrs. Gingrich, just call me.

"Decade-ism" is an ideal sport for the closet misanthrope who wants to remain securely in the closet. Decades are full of people, so if you hurry up and hate the decade just past, you can hate just about everybody now alive, yet be accused of nothing stronger than a sense of history.

—Florence King, *With Charity Toward None*

Man, did the eighties suck. They were almost as bad as the seventies.

Negation:

I haven't been overly fond of the nineties either.

Advertising

> Advertising is the greatest art form of the twentieth century.
>
> —Marshall McLuhan

On August 28, 1922, the first radio commercial was heard on WEAF in New York when the Queensboro Realty Company of Jackson Heights paid $100 for ten groundbreaking minutes of airtime.

Since then, advertising has evolved into something that passes as an art form—at least for those people who see Michelangelo's "David" and say, "I want an ab-isolator," or view Dalí's "Telephone in a Dish with Three Grilled Sardines" and sigh to themselves, "Give me ten minutes and a Vegamatic and you're soup."

Negation:

Today I'll avoid the long lines at the museum by zapping the shows and watching the commercials, shopping channels, and hour-long infomercials. The hairdo in Christina's world...is that held together with old-fashioned pins or did she do that with one hand and a Hairdini? Isn't it a crime that Rubens' models were immortalized and displayed before they had a chance to check out "Buns of Steel"? And Jose Eber's enigmatic smirk...where did I see that before?

Playing baseball for a living is like having a license to steal.
                                                        —Pete Rose

On August 29, 1989, the only major league slugger to refer to his bat as "the daily handle" and the inspiration for "Las Vegas Night" at Reds Stadium, Pete Rose, had his license abruptly revoked when it was announced that he would be banned from baseball for life for betting on professional sports. A year later, he gave his life the royal flush by pleading guilty to charges of tax evasion.

Negation:
Doing what I do for a living is like having a license to grovel.

I always keep a supply of stimulant handy in case I see a snake—which I also keep handy.

—*W. C. Fields*

In Alexandria, Egypt, on this date in 30 B.C., a place and time clearly beyond the reach of Jack Kevorkian, Cleopatra barged into oblivion by committing suicide with an asp.

Negation:
If people kept telling me I looked like Elizabeth Taylor, I'd be suicidal, too.

Vanity dies hard; in some obstinate cases it outlives the man.

—Robert Louis Stevenson

In other obstinate cases, it outlived the calendars that seemed to be keeping track of forum appointments and Bacchanalian festivals perfectly well until some ninny in a toga decided to mess around with it.

August 31st only exists because the emperor Augustus couldn't bear the thought that the month named in his honor was shorter than those named for Janus and Julius. Consequently, he stole a day from February.

Negation:

It doesn't matter who the month is named for. When the first rolls around, collection agents all over the country think of me.

Pigeons: rats with wings.

—Anonymous definition

In his soporific writings, John James Audubon describes a single flock of passenger pigeons that eclipsed the sun for three straight days, passing overhead at a rate of 300 million birds an hour. When they landed, they blanketed an area forty miles long by three miles wide.

Others, whose crops were incinerated by the highly acidic droppings, were equally captivated by the fragile beauty of these airborne petri dishes—and they began to kill them in record numbers. Enterprising hunters spread the ground with alcohol-soaked grain, then whacked huge numbers of drunken birds with clubs.

Yet it wasn't until the early 1800s, when the hunters began to employ "stool pigeons," that the shoots took on an industrial quality. Knowing that pigeons called to each other for help, hunters tied blinded pigeons to stools. When their loyal friends arrived in large flocks, one shot could bring down up to two hundred birds.

That did it. On September 1, 1914, Martha, the last passenger pigeon, died at the Cincinnati Zoo at the age of twenty-nine. She was promptly sent to the Smithsonian for stuffing and display.

Negation:

I don't care if my wife has been chained to a radiator. Find some other pigeon with an acetylene torch.

Ever notice that fifteen minutes into a Jerry Lewis telethon you start rooting for the disease?

—Jim Sherbert

Search if you must through the channels, but you simply cannot get through a Labor Day Weekend without catching a glimpse of the Jerry Lewis telethon.

A heady combination of schmaltz, sweat, and tears, the telethon reminds us of how much stamina, tenacity, and courage it takes to live. It also provides us a sobering reminder of how long it takes washed-up entertainers to die.

—— *Negation:* ——
Like Señor Wences, I will make my last appearance in a box.

One should forgive one's enemies but not before they've been hanged.

–Heinrich Heine

Oliver Cromwell, the murderer of King Charles I, thought he beat the rap when he died of natural causes on this day in 1658. But the monarchy, ever anxious to forgive its enemies, would not be denied its hanging.

In 1661, Cromwell's putrified body was exhumed and hanged from a gibbet (a gibbet is a big forked stick—Norm Abrams could whip one out without even using a router) for six hours. When it was taken down, it was beheaded. The head was then impaled on a pole and displayed in Westminster Hall until 1684. (A longer run than most Broadway musicals.)

Bowed but unbroken, a one-of-a-kind collectible you just don't see on the Home Shopping Club, Cromwell's head bounced through a number of private collections before it fell into the hands of administrators at his alma mater, Sidney Sussex College, Cambridge. It was buried there on March 25, 1960—302 years after its first interment. All in all, a fairly strong argument for cremation.

Negation:

Death is not necessarily the end of my troubles.

All I Really Need to Know I Learned in Kindergarten
                                      —Robert Fulghum's depraved book title

Hey, we been through kindygarden! Curiously, what *we* picked up there—beyond mumps, measles, and various disfiguring pox—never made it into that indefatigably happy, interminable snack-time of a book. Here, then, are the life lessons of the disgruntled, direct from the nursery school of hard knocks:

- ❖ Those who can, sing; those who can't, just mouth the words.
- ❖ To the bully belongs the milk money.
- ❖ The wheels on the bus go round and round—right over your lunch box.
- ❖ Sticks and stones can break one's bones . . . and best of all, they are accessible on any playground.
- ❖ Even if you raise your hand, you may not be allowed to go to the bathroom.
- ❖ He who laughs last is usually the class imbecile.

Negation:

Today I will pay homage to the bright, beautiful, irrepressibly inquisitive kindergartner within me by sticking a pencil up my nostril.

When people around you treat you like a child and pay no attention to the things you say, you have to do something.

—*Lynette A. "Squeaky" Fromme*

Question: If a gun in the middle of a mob of flag-waving Republicans does not fire, does it make a sound?

Answer: Only a squeaky one.

On this date in 1975, a pistol was wrestled away from Manson zombie Lynette A. "Squeaky" Fromme in Sacramento, California, before she could even squeeze off a shot at President Gerald Ford.

At least Sara Jane Moore's gun made some noise when she made her unsuccessful bid to become America's first female assassin in San Francisco on September 22.

────────── *Negation:* ──────────
Attention must be paid.

Equality is not when a female Einstein gets promoted to
assistant professor: Equality is when a female schlemiel
moves ahead as fast as a male schlemiel.

—Ewald Nyquist, NY State Education Commissioner

On this date in 1837, women were granted equal aca-
demic status with male students at Oberlin College.
Among the freedoms granted to women in this groundbreaking mandate were the equal opportunity to read
the Cliff's Notes instead of the book, dead brain-cell
parity under the Frosted-Mug Fairness Act, and the right
to refuse to starch the sheets for the homecoming toga
party.

Negation:
I was a schlemiel before schlemieldom became a political cause or a
lucrative major.

Hope I die before I get old.

—The Who, "My Generation"

Okay, maybe we were wrong . . . some wishes really do come true. Keith Moon fulfilled his hope when he was drummed out of existence on this day in 1978, leaving a corpse that was barely three decades old. In the race toward self-destruction between the two Keiths of the British Invasion, Keith Moon beat Keith Richards hands down and toes up.

Negation:

Today I will be careful what I wish for. I may get it.

Basic research is what I'm doing when I don't know what I am doing.

–Wernher von Braun

Is that supposed to be some sort of insanity defense? Wernher von Braun, head of whichever rocket program was paying the most at the moment, said that his only goal in life was to send a rocket to the moon. On July 20, 1969, he accomplished that goal when the Saturn V— a rocket of von Braun's design—launched men safely to the lunar surface.

But on September 8, 1944, Wernher von Braun was engaged in basic research. The V-2 rockets he launched into the air to fall to earth he knew not where, were raining down on London, imperiling the only source of decent food in all of Britain: Harrods.

Can a scientist be held responsible when his amoral discoveries are used for immoral purposes? Was Wernher as blown away by the V-2 as Londoners were? And who are we to second-guess the methods of a visionary who is reaching for the moon but practicing on intermediate targets—like Big Ben?

— Negation: —

I don't have to be a rocket scientist to justify my screwups—but I can see where it might help.

All happy families resemble one another, but each unhappy family is unhappy in its own way.

—Leo Tolstoy, *Anna Karenina*

The next time you're wallowing in front of a television
talk show, wondering what fetid gene pool could possibly
have spewed forth this misbegotten lineup of bottom-
feeding guests, take a look around your own dinner table.

There's Grandma, whose seat is, once again, suspiciously moist. Cousin Billy, who would never have been
the state swim champion—or the subject of a ten-year
Johns Hopkins inbreeding study—were it not for his
webbed toes. And, of course, there is Aunt Heather,
known previously as Uncle Ernie . . . known currently as
"we're-really-not-connected-by-blood."

Leo Tolstoy, who was born on this day in 1828, knew
familial dysfunction for what it always was: the primor-
dial ooze from which great literature, and unforgettable
holidays spent huddled around the sterno canister, are
spawned. We recommend (since you really have no
choice) that you do the same.

Negation:

Today I will celebrate my uncle, whose jury did not buy the "lonely
shepherd defense," or my sister, who strives in unconventional ways to
satisfy man's universal longing for love.

I have very little patience with the current craze for self-awareness. I am already far too well acquainted with how I feel and frankly, given the choice, I would not. Anyone who is troubled by the inability to feel his or her own feelings is more than welcome to feel mine.

—Fran Lebowitz, *Metropolitan Life*

Of late, therapists have put a lot of effort into getting their paying clients (an insurance policy with a $150,000 mental health care cap is okay, too) to "own" their feelings. Needless to say, all of the really primo feelings—like giddy anticipation, reckless surging passion, unabashed arrogance, blissful satiation, and smug complacency—have already been grabbed up, like the easily identifiable foods on a buffet table.

So what cold, congealed emotional leftovers are left for you to feel? Weary resignation, grim acceptance, a sodden dullness of the spirit, gnawing guilt, tortuously protracted misery only Valerie Bertinelli and a made-for-TV movie could convey, a dark and nameless heaviness, bitter frustration, drooling boredom, crushing disillusionment, and, if it hasn't already been taken by now, trendy numbness.

Negation:
Feel this.

Life is made up of sobs, sniffles, and smiles, with sniffles predominating.

–O. Henry, "The Gift of the Magi"

Sell your hair—your only attractive natural source of warmth (there's not much of a market for cellulite)—to buy some tawdry trifle for your significant other and you're bound to get the sniffles.

O. Henry was born on this date in 1862.

Negation:

If I need to make a down payment on my spouse's large screen, surround-sound, home entertainment center, I'll sell my kidney. I have two of those.

The basic fact about human existence is not that it is a tragedy, but that it is a bore.

—H. L. Mencken, *Prejudices*

The sage of Baltimore was born on this date in 1880. He claimed to have been bored by life, death, the Church, America, FDR, women, men, and especially by the inexorable spread of the booboisie. He would have been bored by you, and us.

As one of our first prominent Germo-American writers, he tried in vain to warn us about the cancer of boredom brought to these shores by his countrymen, those lovers of neat lawns, fresh paint, and marching bands who (here's the frightening bit) make up the largest tile in the ethnic mosaic of America.

Negation: —

During World War II it was legal to kill a German, but kill one now and all hell breaks loose. (Fred Willard, *Fernwood 2-Night*)

Let's see—we've got dirty secrets, conflicting stories, a whole cast of unsavory characters and more overheated media coverage than all of Elizabeth Taylor's marriages put together. Heidi Fleiss? Forget it. It's the Little League World Series I'm talking about.

—Ron Rapoport, *Los Angeles Daily News*

On this date in 1992, the winners of the Little League World Championship—Zamboanga City (Philippines)—were accused of misrepresenting the ages of their players. The team later forfeited the championship when it was discovered that many of the not-so-little-leaguers were over the maximum age of twelve, and that players had been "called up" to Zamboanga from towns up to seven hundred miles away.

In protest, the players refused to shave for a week.

Negation:
Put me in, coach. This bench is hell on my sciatica.

Eternity's a terrible thought. I mean, where's it going to end?

—Tom Stoppard, *Rosencrantz and Guildenstern Are Dead*

Dante Alighieri died on September 14, 1321, a day he had certainly spent enough time anticipating.

Dante's greatest hit is called *The Divine Comedy*, but don't be fooled by the title. A sort of medieval *Who's Who in Hell*, Dante's epic poem is a hierarchical guide to Satan's sulfurous sinkhole that actually ranks sinners by the gravity of their transgressions.

According to Dante, Hell's penthouse is reserved for the relatively benign pagans, who never accepted a religion that offered a get-out-of-eternal-torment-free card. They are followed, in descending order, by gluttons and adulterers, heretics, the violent and suicidal, seducers, panderers and thieves, cheats, skeeves and other lowlifes, liars and wicked counselors, traitors, and finally, His Devilishness, the Prince of Darkness himself.

Although Dante's travelogue is almost seven hundred years old and a tad out-of-date (where, for example, do the syndicators of Rush Limbaugh's television show fit in?), it is by no means passé. Turned upside down, Dante's masterpiece is an organizational chart that can be applied to virtually any major corporation. Used as is, it is a floor plan for a very successful and trendy nightspot.

Negation:

Hell isn't something that's created by a "higher power." Hell is something that's created by an optimistic cook with a can of Spam.

The surest way to make a monkey out of a man is to quote him.

—Robert Benchley

Until we finally looked it up, we always thought that Benchley said that it was the surest way to make *money* from a man, so we started on this little book. It's too late to stop now.

Today is Robert Benchley's birthday.

Negation:

Actually, the surest way to make money from a man is to make a monkey out of him.

Life is a flash of occasional enjoyments lighting up a mass of pain and misery.

—Alfred North Whitehead

For Roy C. Sullivan, "the human lightning conductor of Virginia," even the flashes weren't so hot. The only man known to have been struck by lightning seven times, Sullivan began his attraction for lightning in 1942 when a bolt from the blue blew off his big toenail. When lightning struck twice, in July 1969, Sullivan's eyebrows were sizzled. In July 1970, his left shoulder was fried. On April 16, 1972, his hair was set afire by God's Insta-Match. On August 7, 1972, his new-grown hair was defoliated again. On June 5, 1976, he got his ankle branded. Burned-out, Sullivan went on vacation in June of 1977, where he was promptly zapped while fishing.

By September 1983, Roy Sullivan stopped carrying around his own tree and started carrying a dangerously ungrounded torch. He committed suicide after being rejected in love.

Negation:

It was only a flash in the pan, but heck...I got a charge out of it.

Another thing about my mother that's really intriguing: On the day that Bobby Kennedy was killed, she bought a horse, and then she wanted to name it Sirhan Sirhan, but the Jockey Club wouldn't permit it. Isn't that strange?

—*Patricia Hearst, aka Tanya, on her mother Catherine Hearst's tendency to choose vaguely menacing names*

On this date in 1976, kidnapped newspaper heiress turned Symbionese Liberation Army gun moll Patricia Hearst was captured in a San Francisco apartment. Upon her release from prison, she was picked up in the family car, which her mother called Lee Harvey, driven to the Hearst homestead, also known as Hinckley Hill, where she snacked on Arthur Herman Bremer wafers and soaked up some James Earl Rays.

Negation:
If I had a horse, I'd name it Cinque. (You're welcome.)

Nothing makes me feel as healthy as somebody else's disease.

—Friedrich Aragon

There is nothing like a trip to a sunny clime to bring out the survival instinct in us. This is not because a Florida vacation puts us in proximity to the invigorating sun and surf. It is because it brings us so close to so many who are so near to death.

But where could the eighteenth-century sufferers go to feel better fast? To the bedside of Samuel Johnson—poet, essayist, critic, wit, and placebo—who was born on this date in 1709.

Upon birth Samuel Johnson was thought to be stillborn. Unfortunately, that misconception set the tone for his life. Throughout his adulthood, Johnson suffered from numerous chronic and/or bizarre conditions including asthma, bronchitis, corneal ulcerations, paracusis (the ability to hear only in noisy environments), and edema. To complete the picture, he also had emphysema, extreme flatulence, gallstones, gout, a tendency to collect bodily fluids in the scrotum, and uncontrollable tics of face and limbs.

Although he was also manic-depressive and incontinent, he remained a popular shut-in and an effective remedy for minor aches and pains until his death in 1784.

— Negation: —
I feel better already.

The leading cause of death among fashion models is falling through street grates.

—Dave Barry

Pathologically petite Twiggy entered the world as Leslie Hornby in London on September 19, 1949, weighing only slightly more at birth than she did at the height of her modeling career in the swingin' sixties. The only human being to have been portrayed, full-size, on a cocktail straw, barely living proof of what the typical English diet can do to a person, Twiggy escaped the occupational hazard of the street grate, only to slip through the gap in our collective memory.

Negation:
I couldn't even slip through an open manhole.

Hit at the girl whenever possible.
–Bill Tilden, amateur champion, on how to win at mixed doubles

On September 20, 1973, Billie Jean King met Bobby Riggs in what was billed the "Battle of the Sexes." Riggs promoted the match by squeezing his queen-size macho into a princess-style dress. King promoted the match by squelching rumors of her bisexuality.

In the end, it became clear who to hit at. King won the nationally televised prime-time match in three straight sets.

Negation:
To get the highest TV ratings, hit at the lowest common denominator whenever possible.

Certitude

Yes, Virginia, there is a Santa Claus. He exists as certainly as love and generosity and devotion exist, and you know that they abound and give to your life its highest beauty and joy.

—*New York Sun* editorial, September 21, 1897

But, as our maxed-out credit cards will attest, there is no Santa Claus. What does his nonexistence say about the "certain" existence of love and generosity and devotion? Does a person who believes ever really receive? Or do you have to marry Roseanne Barr to get a Humvee for Christmas?

Negation:

I have the unadulterated faith of an innocent child—and a lien on my house to prove it.

If this is the way Her Majesty treats her prisoners, she doesn't deserve to have any.

—Oscar Wilde

On this day in 1776, Captain Nathan Hale was hanged as a spy by the British. Numerous school-age children have told us that before he went to his death he said, "I only regret that I have but one life to lose for my country." In his shoes, wouldn't we all regret having only one life?

Negation:
Patriotism is a hang-up.

The future is not what it used to be.

–Paul Valéry

The cheerily animated version of Future Shock, *The Jetsons*, aired for the first time on September 23, 1962, giving us our first black-and-white glimpse of the future.

According to the show's producers, *The Jetsons* was set "in the twenty-first century." But you'd never know it from the conveniences that have yet to appear in *our* dreary sky-pads.

Jane Jetson had a Food-A-Rack-A-Cycle. She punched a few buttons and presto! A three-course meal appears on the table and Judy decides against anorexia. We punch a few buttons on the phone and presto! Our Moo Shu Pork is delivered cold to what would be our door . . . if we lived on the next block.

Rosie the Robot cleaned the Jetsons' house with a See-ing-Eye Vacuum cleaner. It had two electronic eyes that searched for dirt. Those who can afford a "Rosie" tell us that their houses are similarly cleaned—by maids with bourbon-enhanced eyes that search for valuables.

To sum up, if you want to meet the real George Jetson, wait until the year 2010 and check the kitchen. He won't be experimenting with cold fusion. He'll be up to his elbows in greasy water, digging what's left of a spoon out of the garbage disposal with a bent fork.

Negation:
Jane, turn off this crazy thing! Jane!

Show me a hero and I will write you a tragedy.
—*F. Scott Fitzgerald, The Crack-Up*

Show us a tragedy and we'll write you a one-liner. Hey, all writers have to have a specialty.

Francis Scott Key Fitzgerald, the Robin Leach of literature, was born in St. Paul, Minnesota, on September 24, 1896. It took a heroic lifelong devotion to writing and drinking to establish his reputation as *the* urban sophisticate of his day and to erase the stigma of his tatty namesake and déclassé birthplace (until we reminded you).

Negation:

I have heroically chosen not to erase the stigma of my déclassé birthplace. But I do wish my grandmother would consider having those tattoos removed.

They fuck you up, your mum and dad.
They may not mean to, but they do.
They fill you up with faults they had
And add some extra, just for you.
                    —Philip Larkin, *This Be the Verse*

We submit this jaunty verse, curiously never adopted by Hallmark, by way of apology—and with some hope that it will hold up as a legal defense when our son (who made us parents on this date) gets old enough to trade in his orthodontic retainer for a legal one.

Alvin Toffler, whom we plan to call as an expert witness, called parenthood "the greatest single preserve of the amateur" (*Future Shock*). We can only hope that our children—and yours—will be able to hire professionals to raise the grandchildren.

Negation:
Parenthood is thankless but not blameless.

Most people can't afford to live where I live. That's why I live there.

— Reggie Jackson

On this date in 1962, a rattletrap 1921 Oldsmobile truck sputtered up the circular drive of a posh Beverly Hills mansion. What spilled out was the mangiest cluster of new neighbors this side of *The Grapes of Wrath*: The only gen-u-ine Ozark hillbilly with good teeth and bad aim. His mother, the only natural predator of the possum. An overactive pituitary gland in stretch-jeans called Jethro. And the family genetic fluke, Donna Douglas. The next thing Milburn Drysdale knew, the old lady was whomping up a mess of roadkill on the patio, the "see-ment pond" was crawling with "critters," and Lester Flatt and Earl Scruggs were reeling around the front gates cranked up on Granny's down-home tonic.

Negation:
The Clampetts could afford to live where I live *before* Jed hit black gold.

People don't choose their careers; they are engulfed by them.

—John Dos Passos

If someone had told you at age twenty that by answering an intentionally vague, three-line want ad with a necessarily vague, three-line résumé, you would determine the course of your life for eight hours of every day, five days a week, for the next thirty-five years, you would have told them to lay off the xerox machine toner. But that's just what happened. And now that xerox machine toner is looking mighty good to you.

That, of course, was the good news. The bad news is that modern corporations take about as much responsibility for their workers as we do for our navel lint. If you've been working your way up in one of the 50% of companies that will downsize this year, you may very soon find yourself engulfed by something even less pleasant than a career.

Negation:
I will clean my navel on company time.

I done it for the wife and kiddies.

—Eddie Cicotte, Chicago "Black Sox" pitcher

On this date in 1920, a grand jury in Chicago indicted eight members of the Chicago White Sox for throwing the 1919 World Series against the Cincinnati Reds (and they didn't even have Pete Rose to blame for it). Although the scandal threw baseball into a temporary slump, it ushered in an era of great excuses, including "I done it to provide Chevy Chase with a schtick" (Gerald Ford); "I done it because you've gotta have heart" (Jeffrey Dahmer); "I done it to see what you get when you mate a football hero with a vacuum cleaner" (Frank Gifford); and our personal favorite, "I done it because a hot dog makes me lose control" (Patty Duke).

Negation:

What little I do, I do out of simple ignorance.

I'm stockpiling Percodan.
> —Buster Poindexter, on the smart pharmaceutical investments that will get him through retirement

In 1982, seven people in the Chicago area retired early and called nobody in the morning after unwittingly taking Extra-Strength Tylenol capsules that had been laced with cyanide. Although the victims were technically headache free with no chance of relapse, 264,000 bottles of the potentially permanent pain reliever were immediately recalled.

Negation:
I've got Tylenol Headache Infinity.

Worms'-Meat, *n.* The finished product of which we are the raw material. The contents of the Taj Mahal, the Tombeau Napoleon and the Grantarium.

—Ambrose Bierce, *The Devil's Dictionary*

It is at least satisfying in some practical sense to think that one day our bodies will give sustenance to a worm, and that the worm will become dinner for some cute little bird, and that the bird will, in turn, be massacred by somebody's cat, and that the cat will eventually be put to sleep by some vet who needs to euthanize at least six pets a week if he's ever going to get the money to pay off the Audi. Unfortunately, the food chain just doesn't work that way anymore. No life form as advanced as a worm can get into a sealed casket. The best we can hope for is that our rotting remains will look good to some single-celled microbes. And that they'll mutate into a new strain of antibiotic-resistant disease that will take over the planet.

Negation:

Be nice to me or I won't make arrangements for cremation.

I'm going to knock the next pitch down your goddamned throat.

> —What Babe Ruth reportedly really said to the pitcher when he "called his shot" in the 1932 World Series

On this date in 1932, brisket-in-cleats Babe Ruth turned his well-documented anger outward (he was as fat and pampered as a veal; who wouldn't be pissed?) and blasted the most famous of his 714 home runs during the World Series at Wrigley Field.

Exactly twenty-nine years later, Ruth's surprisingly slim mortal remains rattled in their casket when Roger Maris hit his sixty-first homer of the 1961 season in Yankee Stadium, squeaking by Ruth's single-season home run record.

Negation:

As the embarrassed ex-fans of Menudo and New Kids on the Block are fond of saying: Records are made to be broken.

I wouldn't want to belong to any club that would accept
me as a member.

—Julius Henry "Groucho" Marx

Groucho was welcomed into the human race in New
York City on this date in 1890. Membership is mandatory
according to civil and religious law. Leaving of your own
volition is punishable only by eternal damnation.

Negation:
Where do I sign up?

I quickly kneel by the side of my bed, thanking God I was raised Catholic since sex will be better because it will always be dirty.

—John Waters, *Crackpot*

In October of 1993, Pope John Paul II released his encyclical on sex and morality, appropriately entitled *Veritatis Splendor.* In it, he proclaimed that "certain acts" (and you know which ones they are) "are intrinsically evil," thus ensuring that sex, at least for Catholics, will remain smutty, lewd, and taboo—but only for procreative reasons.

Negation:
No wonder they call it deathbed conversion.

You can destroy your now by worrying about tomorrow.
—*Janis Joplin*

On the other hand, you can destroy your tomorrows by *not* worrying about tomorrow (Oh, Lord, won't you lease me a Mercedes-Benz for only $599 a month with no money down?), as Janis proved definitively on this day in 1970.

It's one of those no-win situations we're so fond of. Janis Joplin was found dead of a heroin overdose while working on her most successful album, *Pearl*. And six months after her death, on March 20, 1971, she had her first and last number one hit with "Me and Bobby McGee."

Negation:

No one will truly appreciate me until I'm dead. I hope that's not all they appreciate about me.

The art of jumping into trouble without making a splash.
—Art Linkletter, defining diplomacy

On October 5, 1969, the twenty-year-old daughter of TV legend Art Linkletter made her leap to fame . . . from the sixth-floor kitchen window of her Hollywood apartment.

Diane Linkletter's plunge from the zenith of a bad trip to the boulevard of broken dreams was rather undiplomatic—consequently, her LSD-related death made quite a splash. It turned her grieving father from a shameless exploiter of children's mangled locutions into a crusader against their rights to self-medication. It made her name a household word ("Can you get me some of that stuff Diane Linkletter took?") and the center of a philosophical debate ("If Diane Linkletter falls from a tree in the woods, does she leave a trail?"). And it spawned a series of industrial-quality educational films complete with hypnotic pools of swirling colors that made hallucinogens seem a whole lot more interesting to adolescents than that sperm and egg stuff they were serving up in health class.

─────── *Negation:* ───────
Kids do the darnedest things.

I imagined myself as a giant penis launching off from Earth like a spaceship.

–Cary Grant

In the mid-1950s, the Psychiatric Institute of Beverly Hills introduced the beautiful people to an unusual form of chemical therapy based on a little-known drug that "acted as a psychic energizer": LSD. The treatments worked wonders for Grant's wife, Betsy, who began to appreciate the little things in life: Technicolor . . . the confounding complexity of paper . . . water's intriguing tendency to make a person wet. When she noticed that her husband seemed to be on the brink of a nervous breakdown, she invited Cary to drop in and drop out, too.

Before long, Grant was calling Dr. Mortimer Hartman, the supervisor of his cosmic excursions, "My wise Mahatma." He began to share the profoundly meaningful revelations that had come to him in the course of hundreds of trips. ("We should all just smell well and enjoy ourselves more.")

LSD was made illegal on this date in 1966—about the time we all stopped hallucinating about the existence of a suave, debonair chemically unaltered man anywhere on earth.

Negation:

I imagined myself as a giant penis, too... until I started having problems with the blastoff.

Lord, help my poor soul.

> –The last coherent words of Edgar Allan Poe

Forty-year-old poet and Twelve-Step-program back-slider Edgar Allan Poe helped himself out of a hastily scheduled marriage to Sarah Helen Whitman by going on a five-day drinking binge, spending three delirious days at Washington College Hospital in Baltimore, then dying on this date in 1849.

Negation:

The Lord helps those who help themselves. I'll pour.

It is better to light one candle than curse the darkness.
—Christopher Society motto

Rather than curse the darkness, burned-out urban milkmaid Mrs. Catherine O'Leary brought a lantern to her De Koven Street barn on the evening of October 8, 1871, thus enabling her legendary cow to kick off the most destructive fire in American history. By the time it was extinguished, nearly two and a half days later, the Great Chicago Fire had ravaged 2,100 acres and consumed 17,500 buildings (including the fire department's only pumping station). Damage was assessed at 196 million nineteenth-century dollars.

It is interesting to note that although 98,000 were left homeless by the fire, Mrs. O'Leary was not. Her west side home remained miraculously intact. As for the cow, it continued to provide the O'Learys with income. It inspired the first gyro stand.

Negation:

It is no coincidence that the people who light up my life are the same people who burn me up.

I resent performing for fucking idiots who don't know anything.

–John Lennon

John Lennon, who resented performing for you, us, Ed Sullivan, the Queen of England, Brian Epstein, and certainly for adorable mop-top Paul McCartney, was born on this date in 1940.

Negation:
I resent being recognized as a fucking idiot who doesn't know anything.

I swallow well.

—Linda Lovelace

Oh, sure, it's easy to swallow somebody *else's* pride. But as far as the Grand Prix of Gag Suppression goes, what Lovelace could learn from these overachieving omnivores would make her mouth drop open.

According to the *Guinness Book of World Records*, an "insane" woman known as "Mrs. H" holds the record for the greatest quantity of objects ever swallowed by a human being. When the forty-two-year-old began to complain of "slight abdominal pain," doctors discovered that she had ingested 2,533 bits of household clutter, including 947 bent pins which no "insane" person really wants to leave lying around where they could possibly be stepped on.

Not to be outdone, a man in Cape Town, South Africa, sent 212 assorted thingamabobs coursing through his gullet in May of 1985. His cache included fifty-three toothbrushes, two telescopic aerials ("I can't pick up a thing on this radio . . . except maybe my colon"), two whole razors, and 150 disposable razor handles.

Orson Welles, no slouch himself, died on October 10, 1985. There's no telling what he had in his stomach.

Negation:

I've put my foot in my mouth a few times, but since I wasn't wearing two toe rings, a fishing boot, and a pair of spurs it hardly seems worth mentioning.

Two assholes don't make a right.

—Jean Krzanik

But they can make a very fine left-leaning marriage.
This wisdom was passed along to us just before our
wedding by the woman we chose to be our maid of
honor. In Jean's defense, she burped out this quote in
a bar very late at night, but we're proud to adopt it as
the motto for our marriage.

Negation:

If two assholes don't make a right, how do you explain Patrick Buchanan
and Jerry Falwell? Wish us a Happy Anniversary.

Columbus sailed the ocean blue
in fourteen hundred and ninety-two.
> —*A schoolchild's mnemonic device*

Some are born great; some have greatness thrust upon them. But eventually, all of our heroes grate upon us. In our lifetimes, Christopher Columbus has gone from being the greatest dead explorer in world history to the happy inheritor of Leif Eriksson's sloppy seconds, from a rather lame excuse for a parade to the fifteenth-century Donald Trump who destroyed Eden. The 500th anniversary of the voyage he floated (along with several large unpaid loans) passed in 1992 with barely a ripple of enthusiasm.

Negation:

Today, on the anniversary of Columbus' landing on an island fairly close to the continent he is credited with "discovering," I will consider the fading image I'll leave behind when I depart this earth and the myriad ways it will be twisted in the minds of the pitiful few who might—if sufficiently enriched by my demise—occasionally remember me.

They're upbeat, healthy and open about the experience.
I didn't ask them what they were having for dinner.
                    –Frank Marshall, director of the only feel-good movie
                                about cannibalism, *Alive*

On this date in 1972, an airliner carrying the tough,
sinewy, and generally unappetizing members of the Uru-
guayan rugby team crashed in the Andes. Against all
odds, the stalwart survivors overcame gnawing fear and
grinding hopelessness to endure a seventy-day ordeal in
the biting cold.

Those who did not survive became meals that far ex-
ceeded what would have been served on the plane.

Negation:
I am who I eat.

When the going gets tough, the tough get going.

—*Anonymous*

In an effort to avoid hearing Kaye Kyser's jukebox hit, "Ole Buttermilk Sky," Perry Como's fuzzy-wuzzy rendering of "When You Were Sweet Sixteen," and Gene Autry's upbeat warning, "Here Comes Santa Claus," one more time, Chuck Yeager became the first man to fly faster than sound on October 14, 1947.

Negation:
If man ever colonizes the moon, it will be because of Kenny G.

It is with real regret that we learn of Mr. Wayne's recovery from an automobile accident.

—Botched newspaper report (at least, we hope it is)

On October 15, 1966, an unnamed seventy-five-year-old driver (we like to think it was Mr. Wayne) in McKinney, Texas, received ten traffic tickets, drove on the wrong side of the road four times, committed four hit-and-runs, and caused six accidents, all within a twenty-minute time span.

--- Negation: ---
If you don't like the way old people drive, stay off the sidewalk.

Monsieur, I beg your pardon. I did not do it on purpose.
> —*Marie Antoinette*, apologizing for stepping on her
> executioner's toe, October 16, 1793

Yes, she did.

Negation:

I beg your pardon. I did not mean to knock you down the subway stairs then kneel on your testicles while giving you unnecessary CPR with both fists.

We all agree that pessimism is a mark of superior intellect.
—John Kenneth Galbraith

Only the man who finds everything wrong and expects it to get worse is thought to have a clear brain.
—John Kenneth Galbraith

When the Stock Market fell 508 points on Monday, October 17, 1987, most people acted surprised, though some experts boasted after the fact that they knew it was going to happen (they just didn't want to tell us tycoons with ten inherited shares of Passé Technologies and scare us into panic selling). Really, we only remember John Kenneth Galbraith predicting the historic market "correction" the day before it turned so many "haves" into "used-to-haves." Better yet, he actually *wished* it on us, saying that the market *deserved* to do a Hindenburg simply because of its bloat—and for its lighter-than-air basis in Ronald Reagan's dumber-than-dirt economics.

Negation:
Now I understand the meaning of Schadenfreude!

Wee, sleekit, cow'rin, tim'rous beastie,
O what a panic's in thy breastie.
—Robert Burns, *To a Mouse*

On this date in 1969, the Department of Health, Education, and Welfare identified the "panic" in the "breasties" of otherwise healthy laboratory animals as cancer brought on by the overuse of the artificial sweeteners known as cyclamates. They were immediately fitted with silicone breast implants, given a red dye #2 chaser, and put out of their misery.

Negation:
At least I'm not being used as a human guinea pig. Where'd you say I left my cellular phone?

This is going to hurt you a lot more than it will hurt me.
—*Anonymous parent*

A professor at Eton College may have broken a record—and several very well-made paddles—when he whipped seventy boys, one after another, in a single day in the 1800s. Although it is unknown whether the professor ever really got to the bottom of the boys' educational difficulties, he injured himself so badly in the process that he suffered incapacitating body aches for more than a week.

To prevent similar work-related injuries, the U.S. Supreme Court handed down its decision on corporal punishment on this date in 1975, ruling that teachers could spank students but only if students were told in advance of the behaviors that would merit physical correction. Don't say you haven't been warned.

Negation:

Spare the rod and protect your golf swing.

She's got to learn to reconcile herself to being Mrs. Aristotle Onassis because the only place she'll find sympathy from now on is in the dictionary between shit and syphilis.
—*Aristotle Socrates Onassis*

She may have been a little confused as to where, exactly, to find sympathy, but the Queen of Camelot certainly honed in on inheritance. Although the vaguely rhinocerotic Aristotle Onassis somehow missed it, it was right there in Webster's all the time, wedged cozily between incontinence and irregular respiration.

Oh, sure, there were some who were repulsed when Jackie Kennedy stooped to wed her shady shipping magnate on October 20, 1968 (though neither of us personally know any women in our circle who would turn down a marriage proposal from a billionaire with a limited life expectancy). But she regained the world's sympathy when she regained her widowhood, moved to a city where Regis Philbin is hailed as a celebrity, and took up the world's most thankless profession: book editor.

Negation:

The universal sympathy of a grieving nation and fifty cents used to be able to buy you a cup of coffee.

There is no denying the fact that writers should be read but not seen. Rarely are they a winsome sight.

—Edna Ferber

On this date in 1969, Beat generation speed typist and armchair epicure Jack Kerouac was found dead at the age of forty-seven. He was fatally stricken with *something* (probably the realization that he would one day be the prototype for Charles Kuralt) while drinking heavily, eating tuna fish out of the can, and watching *The Galloping Gourmet* on the Zenith.

Negation:

That Graham Kerr. He really kills me.

The world was created on 22d October, 4004 B.C. at 6 o'clock in the evening.
—James Ussher, Archbishop of Armagh, *Annals of the World* (1654)

Who would dare challenge such a precise, authoritatively delivered and maybe even divinely inspired calculation? For two hundred years, nobody. Then, in 1859, Dr. John Lightfoot of the University of Cambridge popped up to inform the world that the actual date of its Creation was October 23rd, 4004 B.C., at nine in the morning. According to him, Ussher was off by a whole fifteen hours.

Unfortunately, the only thing created on *this* date was the idea that nothing seems more unchallengeable than an exact calculation.

Negation:
The world will end on...I'll pick an exact time and date, rent a billboard, and start my own lucrative religious cult.

Democracy means people of all races, creeds, and colors working hard so they can move away from people of all races, creeds, and colors.

—Johnny Carson

Whe-e-e-ere's Johnny? Born on this date in 1925, the king of scripted geniality and defender of democracy lives in nearly total isolation in Malibu, California.

Negation:

I have cleverly parlayed a lifetime of hard work into a lifetime of squalor. The only danger in becoming a recluse is that no one will notice I am gone.

Stubbornness: To cut off one's nose to spite one's face.
                                    —*Publilius Syrus, Sententiae*

If you've been nosing around to discover the name of the chronic drip that inspired this cliché about stubbornness, look no further than the abbreviated septum of Tycho Brahe, Danish astronomer. A man who would sooner yield a body part than an argument, Brahe literally lost his nose in a duel with a fellow student over a math problem. He then spited his face by replacing his cropped proboscis with a prosthesis made of gold and silver.

Did that experience cut down on his mulish behavior? No. But this one did. On October 13, 1601, Brahe was invited to dine at the home of a Czech baron. Although he had urinary problems and neglected to relieve himself before leaving home, he spent the rest of the evening drinking heavily. Unwilling to show bad manners by heeding the call of nature, Brahe sat steadfast at the table until his bladder burst.

Determined to prove himself even more unyielding than his bladder, Brahe lingered eleven days until septicemia broke the deadlock on October 24th.

Negation:
I think I'll skip dessert.

When I was a child my mother said to me, "If you become a soldier you'll be a general. If you become a monk you'll end up as the pope." Instead I became a painter and wound up as Picasso.

–Pablo Picasso

Pablo Picasso, who became a multimillionaire by producing paintings that did not become his subjects, was born on this date in 1881.

Those who take the sword perish by the sword, and those
who don't take the sword perish by smelly diseases.
                                        —George Orwell

In the last week of October 1918, flu claimed the lives
of 21,000 Americans. By the time the contagion had run
its course, over 550,000 Americans—more than ten times
the battle casualties sustained in World War I—had gone
from diseased to deceased. The point here is obvious:
Since the worst you can catch in the trenches is a bullet,
it can be safer to join the war of the moment than to
dodge the draft.

--- *Negation:* ---
My peaceful life is a petri dish teeming with pestilence.

Being a woman is of special interest to aspiring male transsexuals. To actual women it is simply a good excuse not
to play football.

—Fran Lebowitz, *Metropolitan Life*

There are people (chubby, pink British diplomats who'll
take any port in a storm among them) who claim that
they simply cannot distinguish an aspiring male transsexual from an actual woman. To prevent further confusion, and to discourage the writing of dramas that
make us rethink the fairly straightforward issue of gender, we provide the following guidelines: Anyone who
lets her leg hair grow in the winter is an actual woman.
Anyone who has purchased and used an Epilady is an
aspiring male transsexual. When actual women forget to
take their pill they get children. When aspiring male
transsexuals forget to take their pill they still get to go
to the Lavender Ball—but as Martha Rae. In brief, you
can always tell the aspiring male transsexual in the
crowd. She's the one wearing a skirt.

Frances Ann "Fran" Lebowitz, an actual woman who
has never been photographed wearing anything but trou-
sers, was born in Morristown, New Jersey, on this date
in 1950.

Negation:
Bend my gender and I'll bend yours.

. . . the Statue of Liberty, that archetypal manifestation of the national yearning for kitsch. Its torch that *actually lights up* provides that novelty feature of pseudo-literalism that always excites lovers of BAD.

–Paul Fussell, *Bad or, the Dumbing of America*

The lava lamp in New York harbor was dedicated on this date in 1886—a time when visitors could still climb right up Lady Liberty's skirt then zip straight up her arm like a tetanus booster.

Of course, nobody saw any real kitsch until the statue's hundredth birthday in 1986 when our own French-woman-that-can't-cook was rededicated by Ronald Reagan, Liza Minnelli, hundreds of synchronized Elvis Presley impersonators, a 40,000-piece fireworks extravaganza, and the kind of David Wolper hi-jinx that mean freedom to me.

------ Negation: ------

I can't wait until the Great Wall of China celebrates its 2200th birthday in a few years. Get a few hundred of those acrobats juggling tables with their feet, hang a few strings of those red chili-pepper lights on that sucker, and it'll be something to see.

> . . . the race is not to the swift, nor the battle to the strong, neither yet bread to the wise, nor yet riches to men of understanding, nor yet favor to men of skill; but time and chance happeneth to them all.
>
> —Ecclesiastes 9:11

Now, we don't mean this blasphemously, but the Bible is a lot like the *Reader's Digest*. Both are compilations of insights submitted by authors whose qualifications are known only to God. Both are carefully edited to reflect a two-thousand-year-old sensibility. Yet unlike the *Reader's Digest*, the Bible can actually enlighten on issues pertinent to modern life—with a few revisions.

Though some things do change in a couple of millennia, it is reassuring to note that the race is still not to the swift: it is generally to the driver with the best corporate sponsorship. The battle these days is usually won by the side with the highest paid lawyers. The lawyers, by the way, also get most of the bread. And the riches? They remain the exclusive domain of those born with a seven- or eight-figure hereditary head start program.

As for time and chance, they still happeneth to us all . . . but it's nothing a good plastic surgeon can't undo.

Negation:

The race is not always to the swift, nor that battle to the strong—but that's the way to bet. (Damon Runyon)

Poets, like whores, are only hated by each other.
—William Wycherley

To prove this, we include a sampling of poetic potshots taken, not by the blockheaded public or envious critics, but by each other.

She was the Judy Garland of American poetry.
—James Dickey on Sylvia Plath
No more Keats, I entreat: flay him alive; if some of you don't, I must skin him myself.
—Lord Byron
His poetry is not even trash.
—Karl Shapiro on Rod McKuen
In the case of many poets, the most important thing to do . . . is to write as little as possible.
—T. S. Eliot
Go swallow a bottle of Coke and let it fizz out your ears.
—William Carlos Williams to Ezra Pound

Ezra Pound, the only confirmed looney in this entire entry, was born in Hailey, Idaho, in 1885.

Negation:

I used to write a little poetry myself. Then I found out that the windows at the McDowell artists colony weren't fitted with bullet-proof glass.

Nobody ought to wear a Greek fisherman's cap who doesn't meet two qualifications:
1. He is Greek.
2. He is a fisherman.

–Roy Blount, Jr.

What frightens us on Halloween isn't the spectre of roving bands of four-foot extortionists dressed as blood-sucking ghouls and frenzied escapees from Bedlam. It is the certain knowledge that, at least tonight, they have not come in costume.

Negation:

I would dress as one of the living dead this Halloween, but that would be redundant.

I went to a fight the other night and a hockey game broke out.

–Rodney Dangerfield

The Boston Bruins was the first American team admitted to the National Hockey League on November 1, 1924. One of three significant Canadian imports (along with outmoded human air-raid siren Neil Young and those irritating coins that look like money but spend like bingo chips), hockey has skyrocketed in popularity in this country, not just because it is a game of strength and artistry on ice, but because it is the only place you can go to watch white guys fight.

──── *Negation:* ────
I went to a Sexaholics Anonymous meeting the other night and a baseball game broke out.

TV—chewing gum for the eyes.

–Frank Lloyd Wright

On this date in 1959, the overinflated ratings bubble blew up in the faces of TV game show producers when Charles Van Doren confessed to a congressional subcommittee that he had deceived his friends ("and I have millions of them") by agreeing to be fed the jackpot-winning answers to the popular prime-time game show, *Twenty-One*.

Among the other surprise winners of television's intellectual era were Dr. Joyce Brothers, who took home $64,000 after answering an obscure question about boxing (!), and a civil service employee who credited his photographic memory for his record $264,000 winnings— yet could not work as a census taker because he couldn't read the maps.

Negation:

I'm not worried about the people who had to cheat to win *The $64,000 Question*. I'm worried about the people who have to cheat to outwit a wooden-headed puppet on *Hollywood Squares*.

There is but one truly serious philosophical problem, and that is suicide.

—Albert Camus, *The Myth of Sisyphus*

There is but one truly serious philosophical problem, and that is the philosopher. Longer-winded than a giraffe with gas, about as crucial to the burning issues of the day as a condom at a weenie roast, philosophers go on and on about the darnedest things . . . the limits of thought . . . what it means to Be . . . and most annoying, nothing at all, as evidenced by this excerpt from a book by Jean-Paul Sartre:

The Being by which Nothingness arrives in the world is a being such that in its Being, the Nothingness of its Being is in question. *The being by which Nothingness comes to the world must be its own Nothingness . . .*

—Jean-Paul Sartre, *Being and Nothingness*

Don't you just want to shake him and say, "Look, it's nothing, okay?"

Anyway, we're not surprised Camus felt the need to boil everything down to a single sentence. And we're really not surprised that that sentence contained the word suicide, either.

Negation:

I have nothing to fear but Nothing itself.

Do not go gentle into that good night.
Rage, rage against the dying of the light.
—Dylan Thomas, *Do Not Go Gentle into that Good Night*

Is the bloody man dead yet?
—Caitlin Thomas at St. Vincent's Hospital, November 1953

If he'd been able to speak in his last days, Dylan Thomas might have buzzed the nurse for a little less rage at the dying of *his* light.

On November 4, the appropriately initialed D.T. was taken to a New York hospital in a not-uncharacteristic alcohol-induced coma brought on by the ingestion of eighteen straight whiskeys. Although his doctors did all they could, including administering a drug that might have precipitated fatal breathing difficulties, Thomas lapsed into his final sleep. It would not be undisturbed.

On the evening of November 8, Thomas's estranged wife Caitlin arrived at St. Vincent's, shrieking the demoralizing quote given above. She proceeded to bite the hospital attendant, rip a crucifix from the wall, and fight with assorted bystanders before being subdued.

For her trouble, Caitlin Thomas got a rubber room in a private clinic overlooking the East River. And Dylan Thomas got what he wished for, a noisy end.

─────── *Negation:* ───────
And people complain about hospital visitors who sit on the edge of the
bed.

A new scientific truth does not triumph by convincing its opponents and making them see the light, but rather because its opponents eventually die, and a new generation grows up that is familiar with it.

–Max Planck, *Scientific Autobiography*

This doesn't just work for scientific truths. Death is the only thing that ends any argument, be it marital (remember Dylan and Caitlin?), congenital (*see* Chang and Eng, January 17), or paraprofessional (Don't bother looking anything up. Just think of any artist and stare into the nearest gutter).

Any other silences at the ends of arguments are simply seething resentments and quiet grudges.

Negation:

How many people are looking forward to my funeral as the perfect opportunity to get in the last word?

Serious sport has nothing to do with fair play. It is bound up with hatred, jealousy, boastfulness, disregard of all rules and sadistic pleasure in witnessing violence; in other words it is war minus the shooting.

–George Orwell, *The Sporting Spirit*

On this date in 1869, Rutgers beat Princeton six to four in the first intercollegiate football game. Some say it wasn't really football, because players were not allowed to run with the ball and there were twenty-five boys on each squad. But college football turned out to be an entertaining substitute for the Civil War, which ended in overtime in 1865, and it gave style-conscious New Jersey schoolboys a chance to wear helmets long before they came into vogue—on the battlefields of World War I.

Negation:

Today I will ask myself: If football is war minus the shooting, is hockey Armageddon plus a puck?

Yoghurt. Has it been made with radium or mesothorium?
— Marie Curie, apparently tired of a bland diet, on her deathbed in 1934

Marie Sklodowska Curie, better known for her discovery of radioactivity than for her distinctive touch with dairy products, was born on this day in 1867. Without Madame Curie, humankind might have been spared the development of the X-ray machine—and the certain knowledge that our insides look even worse than our outsides do.

—— Negation: ——
I will have my chest x-rayed.

Damn the great executives, the men of measured merriment, damn the men with careful smiles . . . oh, damn their measured merriment.

—Sinclair Lewis, *Arrowsmith*

You must . . . dissemble in order to effect the kind of personality—artificially warm but never actually friendly—that suits the corporate culture.

—Barbara Ehrenreich, *The Worst Years of Our Lives*

What would the office be without enforced civility, faux familiarity, compulsory collegiality, synthetic sensitivity, and measured merriment? It'd be home. And you can't beg, borrow, or steal a distantly jovial round of golf from that crew.

Negation:

The bad news is I can't be myself at work. The good news is neither can anybody else.

Joan is as good as my lady in the dark.

—Duchess of Newcastle

Then again, after thirteen hours in a pitch-black elevator, even the call box starts to take on a certain *je ne sais quoi*.

On this date in 1965, the malfunction of an automatic relay device at a generating plant near Niagara Falls caused a massive power blackout over an 80,000-square-mile area of the Northeast. New York, most of New England, parts of New Jersey, Pennsylvania, Ontario, and Quebec, were cast into darkness for up to thirteen hours.

Nine months later, the affected states and provinces experienced a population boomlet. The resulting infants were dubbed "blackout babies."

Negation:

My blackouts are too frequent to make history and too enjoyable to produce babies.

It's not easy being green.

—Kermit the Frog

And it isn't any easier being yellow, judging from the mishaps that have befallen Wayne Quinn, 6'6" poultry-on-the-spot and Big Bird impersonator.

The scenario seemed harmless enough. Quinn would portray PBS's most recognizable pullet at a four-year-old's Braintree, Massachusetts, birthday party. But when he made his way, in costume, from the company van to the party, he was accosted by a group of six youths whose language seemed to have been brought to them by the letter F.

Nor did the belligerent Birdketeers disperse after the party. When Quinn emerged, the teenagers punched him in the beak, kicked him about the wing and gullet sections, and tenderized him generally with a baseball bat. The teenagers were later arraigned on charges ranging from simple assault to assault and battery with a dangerous weapon.

On November 10, 1969, the only urban neighborhood with no crime rate, *Sesame Street*, moved into the nirvana established by Mister Rogers on PBS stations from coast to coast. Together the shows brainwashed our children into believing that it might actually be safe to walk out the front door.

Negation:
If I were Bert, I'd be watching my pigeon-keeping, bottle-cap collecting, polyester ass, too.

For what can war but endless war still breed?

—John Milton

It's Armistice Day. The eleventh hour of the eleventh day of the eleventh month of the eighteenth year of the twentieth century was the hour on which the Germans signed the armistice, thus officially ending the "war to end all wars." The eleventh of November was supposed to remain a hallowed day forever.

Of course, "forever" is always negotiable. Other wars followed and Armistice Day was deconsecrated. Renamed Veterans Day, it eventually became the last day of a wasted three-day weekend.

Veterans Day is traditionally marked by the ritualized laying of credit cards at department store counters.

Negation:

Today I will take a ruthless mental inventory of all of the wondrous—and therefore unattainable—things that have been promised to me forever or in perpetuity.

The books we need are the kind that act upon us like a misfortune, that make us suffer like the death of someone we love more than ourselves, that make us feel as though we were on the verge of suicide, or lost in a forest remote from all human habitation—a book should serve as an ax for the frozen sea within us.

—Franz Kafka

We hope we've done our job.

Negation:

Today I will consider the breadth, scope, and far-reaching cultural significance of this groundbreaking, transformational tome and wonder what, if anything, publishers actually reject.

Just because I'm happy doesn't mean I'm shallow.
                    —Kathie Lee Gifford, *I Can't Believe I Said That!*

Oh, yes, it *does*. But that doesn't mean that cruise-line harpy and Mattel Vacu-Form escapee Kathie Lee doesn't encourage those around her to plumb the depths—with or without rubber gloves.

As she relates in her mega-selling paean to thoughtful self-examination, *I Can't Believe I Said That!*, Kathie Lee was dressed to the nines for a Miss America Pageant photo session (a sure sign of a profound and far-ranging intellectual life) and her wrist had just been adorned with a costly sample of a sponsor's jewelry when nature, rather than PBS depth-finder Bill Moyers, called. Pro that she is, Kathie Lee made a quick pit stop and returned to the shoot—only to discover that the bracelet had slipped from her wrist.

Gathering up her assistant, Mickey, she quickly hurried back to the ladies' room and inspected the porcelain convenience. Sure enough, there was something bright and yellow in the depths of the bowl and it wasn't last night's corn. To make a long story short and a shallow anecdote even shallower, *somebody* dragged the latrine and fished the bracelet out—and it wasn't the person who had dropped it in.

On this date, whichever day it may be, in this year, whichever year it may be, Kathie Lee is on television.

Negation:
I'm up to my elbows in somebody else's depth.

I just want to be normal.

—Prince Charles

Prince Charles, who talks to flowers, wishes to be reincarnated as a tampon, and reportedly sleeps with the tattered sleeve of a robe given to him twenty years ago by Camilla Parker-Bowles, was born on this date in 1948.

Many people find smoking objectionable. I myself find
many—even more—things objectionable. I do not like
aftershave lotion, adults who roller-skate, children who
speak French, or anyone who is unduly tan. I do not,
however, go around enacting legislation and putting up
signs.

—Fran Lebowitz, *Social Studies*

On November 15, 1492, Christopher Columbus noted in
his journal that the natives indigenous to the "new
world" he discovered were smoking tobacco. Since then,
the presence of smokers has been noted primarily by
people who'll object to virtually anything—motherhood,
the Statue of Liberty, and one-legged veterans—if it gets
them a better table at a popular restaurant.

Frankly, we can think of many potential tablemates
who are more objectionable than a smoker. A diner who
picks his teeth—while holding them in his hand—at the
table. Any restaurant-goer who spent the afternoon dis-
assembling a carnival tilt-a-whirl. Do we demand that
miscreants be isolated in separate sections? Not while
salmonella is a potential source of passive retribution.

Columbus made his second greatest discovery—
recreational smoking—in mid-November. Alas, these are
Columbus- and smoker-bashing times. The middle of the
month is now reserved for the Great American Smokeout
sponsored by the American Cancer Society.

Negation:
I will annoy self-righteous strangers even if it kills me.

Our parents were of Midwestern stock and very strict. They didn't want us to grow up to be spoiled and rich. If we left our tennis rackets out in the rain, we were punished.

—Nancy Ellis, sister of George Bush

The Society to Prevent Cruelty to Children was founded in 1875 by Henry Bergh and Elbridge T. Gerry. Based upon Bergh's pet project, the Society to Prevent Cruelty to Animals, the organization became an unwavering opponent of such abuses as child labor, corporal punishment—and unfair demands to tend to the lowly tasks that were better suited to the help.

Negation:
In my family, nobody even noticed when I was left out in the rain.

History, a distillation of rumor.
> —Thomas Carlyle, *History of the French Revolution*

Go right to the source and ask the horse,
He'll give you the answer that you'll endorse . . .
> —Theme from *Mister Ed*

Most of us know (or think we know) only one thing about Catherine the Great of Russia, and it concerns this day in 1796: that is, the date of her death.

There is no dispute that Catherine had the voracious sexual appetites of a farm animal. Her well-documented affairs with scores of men prove that "neigh" wasn't in her vocabulary. And there is no argument that the sixty-seven-year-old ruler had visited with her current (twenty-seven-year-old) lover only hours before her fatal stroke. But there is absolutely no evidence to support the rumor that that lover had four legs instead of the customary two; that Catherine the Great had a "thing" for any stud with alfalfa on his breath and lasix in his belly; or that she was inadvertently crushed when the harness which suspended her partner above her bed proved unable to hold her horses.

Where, oh where, do these ugly stories start? Rumor has it that the tale was widely circulated in the early 1960s—and that it was traced to a stable behind the home of a secretive architect named Wilbur Post.

Negation:
When you've had enough, just say "whinny."

You are a pest, by the very nature of that camera in your hand.

—Princess Anne

By the time the average American child born today reaches his or her eighteenth birthday, he or she will have been the subject of an average of 120 hours of videotape; 1,650 "candid" ("Just blow out the candles one more time, okay?") snapshots; fourteen class pictures (one cute, one toothless, five sullen, one in which your child mysteriously appears wearing clothing he or she does not own, five you will attribute to that "awkward age," and one group shot in which your child is sneezing); sixteen department store portraits taken against a background that is copyright by Timothy Leary; and nine team or club portraits documenting his or her passing interest in baseball, karate, sumo wrestling, and animal husbandry. How did we come to calculate these statistics? What else have we got to do? People refuse to visit us anymore.

Louis "Say *fromage!*" Daguerre, father of the photograph, was born on this date in 1789 (just in case you're looking for someone to blame).

Negation:

My life is a series of Kodak moments: underdeveloped, overexposed, with all the best parts cut off.

Self-esteem, *n.* An erroneous appraisement.
— Ambrose Bierce, *The Devil's Dictionary*

Once upon a time, you had to be either Alfred Nobel or Alfred E. Newman to sincerely feel good about yourself. Now self-esteem—and its warm and fuzzy derivative, monoxodil—is available to just about everybody. Consequently, victims esteem their victimhood, criminals esteem their criminality, and, as Susan Sontag pointed out in *Death Kit*: "He who despises himself esteems himself as a self-despiser."

Negation:

My self-esteem is illusory—but I can still pat myself on the back for realizing it.

The Puritan hated bear-baiting, not because it gave pain to the bear, but because it gave pleasure to the spectators.
—Thomas Babington Macaulay, *History of England*

I'm not a vegetarian because I love animals; I'm a vegetarian because I hate plants.
—A. Whitney Brown

The taste-bud-atrophied producers of fat-free foods aren't trying to free you from cardiac arrest; they're trying to free you from your money. The corporation you work for isn't concerned with their ability to provide you with an income; they're concerned with your ability to provide them with an income. And curmudgeons aren't grumpy because they abhor levity; they're grumpy because levity abhors them.

Negation:

Today I will drink until I see double, not because I am addicted to alcohol, but because I want to recycle two bottles.

No matter what she does, she remains, in the eyes of the media and celebrity watchers, the Lorna Luft of the upper classes.

> —Society writer Taki on the not-quite-Jackie ripple in the Bouvier gene-pool, Lee Radziwill

Same genes, different day. But as Liza Minnelli would be too glad to belt out, what a difference a day makes! If not for a gestational head start and a little paternity mix-up, *she'd* be Lorna Luft.

As Alec Baldwin, Billy Baldwin, and what's-his-name Baldwin prove, there is at least one Lorna Luft in every family. Sylvester Stallone is a star. Frank Stallone is a related incident. Michael Douglas got his father's cleft chin. Joel, Peter, Vincent, Eric, and Anthony Douglas got in the wrong line when they gave out the recognizable facial deformities. Jeff and Beau Bridges might seem like Lorna Lufts to us—but not to their unknown sister. As for Roger Clinton, he would have been a Lorna Luft even if he had been an only child.

Lorna Luft who, no matter what she does, will remain the Lee Radziwill of Flatbush, was born on this date in 1953.

Negation:

In my family, my sister was the smart one. My brother was the pretty one. I was the other one.

Do you realize the responsibility I carry? I'm the only one standing between Nixon and the White House.

—*John F. Kennedy to his brother just prior to the 1960 election*

If you are old enough to recall your exact whereabouts when you confronted the unthinkable, we don't have to tell you what happened on November 22, 1963. And if you are honest enough to evaluate your exact whereabouts today, you also know what happened thereafter.

Negation:

The only thing standing between me and the chronic five o'clock shadow of my fears is time.

Education: the inculcation of the incomprehensible into the indifferent by the incompetent.

—John Maynard Keynes

American Education Week is celebrated the Sunday through Saturday preceding the fourth Thursday of the month—a date that cannot be accurately pinpointed by 98% of the publicly educated population.

Negation:

I will begin my celebration of American Education Week when everybody else does: the instant the bus pulls up to the curb in September.

There are three kinds of lies: lies, damned lies, and statistics.

—Benjamin Disraeli

Statistics are important . . . to statisticians. If not for America's compulsive need to quantify life's minutiae, statisticians would have to find something to fall back on, like a teaching job or a bayonet. But as busy as these endlessly curious factoid collectors seem to be, they never seem to compile statistics on the things that matter to you most. Things like:

❖ The chances of finding the twenty-dollar bill you put into the pocket of your coat ten minutes ago 3%

❖ The chances that your mother will find the leather S&M mask with the zippered mouth you were given as a shower gift nine years ago and haven't seen since 88%

❖ The probability that piano lessons will turn your child into another Mozart 0.000000002%

❖ The probability that piano lessons will turn your child into another Marvin Hamlisch . . . . better than you think

----

Negation:
There's only one thing that I have a 100% probability of experiencing, and it isn't taxes.

We hold these truths to be self-evident, that all men are created equal, that they are endowed by their Creator with certain unalienable Rights, that among these are Life, Liberty and the pursuit of Happiness.

–The Declaration of Independence

Some of us are more easily alienated from these natural rights than others. Consider Lawrence Hanratty, referred to in the press as "the unluckiest guy in New York"—a respectable title in a state with a death penalty.

Nearly electrocuted on a construction site in 1984, Hanratty tried to sue for damages after waking up from a coma with permanent damage to his heart and liver. His first lawyer was disbarred; two other lawyers died on him. His wife hired an attorney of her own and ran off with him. By that time, the statute of limitations on his case had expired.

Hanratty lapsed into a second coma in 1989 which gave him several weeks of peace. In 1994, his car was demolished by "an errant driver" in the Bronx. After police left the scene, he was robbed of $250 by a kid with a gun. In 1995, his landlord tried to evict him. Through it all, Hanratty has been hooked up to oxygen, taken forty-two pills a day, and has been denied Medicaid, Social Security, and welfare.

Lawrence Hanratty has had something happen to him on nearly every date for the past twelve years.

--- Negation: ---
If he had spilled a cup of McDonald's coffee in his lap, he could have been a millionaire.

Still she haunts me, phantomwise,
Alice moving under skies
Never seen by waking eyes.

–Lewis Carroll, *Through the Looking-Glass*

Gone are the days when a math teacher's sexual obsession with young girls could result in literary masterpieces (and the occasional nude photo taken with a mother's permission) rather than jail time or banishment. So, let's commemorate this day in 1864, when Charles Dodgson sent "Alice's Adventures Under Ground" to twelve-year-old Alice Pleasance Liddell as an early Christmas present.

Negation:

We are but older children, dear, / Who fret to find our bedtime near.

Born in a hotel room—and God damn it—died in a hotel room!

—Eugene O'Neill's last words

Eugene O'Neill, dramatist and lifelong TB sufferer, stiffed the celestial bellhop on this date in 1953. The playwright died too soon to collect his last Pulitzer Prize. He made his long day's journey into night three years before his play of the same name was produced. Nor did he get a crack at the "Booby Prize." Marilyn Monroe married his lucky colleague, Arthur Miller, in 1956.

Negation:

Born in a hospital—and God damn it—I'll die in a hospital.

Finally in New York, a stabbing we can all feel good about.

—Jay Leno, commenting on the untimely demise of the Barney balloon, punctured by a lamppost during the 1994 Macy's Thanksgiving Day Parade

THE TOP FOUR THINGS (OTHER THAN THE DEFLATION OF BARNEY) YOU CAN BE THANKFUL FOR ON THANKSGIVING DAY

4. Your lowlife neighbor did not scrape together enough money out of his monthly disability check to buy yet another rusting hulk, have it towed to a position of prominence on his front lawn and put up on blocks so you could watch the nesting habits of vermin and oxidation of metal over time.
3. The fact that turkey is one of the three foods that don't give Uncle Stanley gas.
2. Here, at last, is a meal Grandpa can't eat with his teeth out.
1. The Thanksgiving Day meal—the only remaining politically incorrect dinner still served up unapologetically laden with fat, salt, and nitrites, just the way normal people who would be satisfied with a normal life span like it.

--- Negation: ---

For things that have not yet happened and illnesses I do not yet have, I am truly grateful.

As for the pyramids, there is nothing to wonder at in them so much as the fact that so many men could be found degraded enough to spend their lives constructing a tomb for some ambitious booby, whom it would have been wiser and manlier to have drowned in the Nile, and then given his body to the dogs.

—Henry David Thoreau, *Walden*

What are the lives of a few thousand expendable slaves compared to the preservation of mummified monarchs, golden prostheses, and jewel-encrusted doodads? Or, to give the question a more contemporary appeal, what are the lives of a few million expendable twentieth-century corporate lackeys compared to the preservation of ossified CEOs, golden parachutes, and the managers-only coffeepot?

On November 29, 1922, Lord Carnavon and Howard Carter discovered Tutankhamen's tomb, proving that it's never too late for an ambitious booby to come out of retirement.

--- Negation: ---

I am digging a grave for myself while building a pyramid that belongs to someone else.

This wallpaper is killing me; one of us has got to go.
                                        —The last words of Oscar Wilde

Oscar Wilde, pushed to the wall by cerebral meningitis, found that wall covered with scrubbable but unstrippable gold-flocked fleur-de-lis scattered on a shimmering field of puce papier peint set off by a peeling maladie de la vigne border. He died of ornamental causes in (where else?) Paris on November 30, 1900, at the age of 46.

Negation:

My decorator said my walls should reflect the way I really live, so I got them plastered.

Fire is inspirational. They should use it in the Olympics.
'Cause I did the fifty-yard dash in three seconds.

—Richard Pryor

The history of human advancement is not traced by the development of life-altering conveniences like hair-in-a-can or the evolution of art (although nothing has done more for the technique of airbrushing than the unbidden-comebacks of Nancy Sinatra), but by man's continuing discovery of new and inspiring uses for fire.

So what if Neanderthal man knocked two rocks together and lit the first fart? Formerly hot comic Richard Pryor lit a fire under his career and incinerated it! And big deal if NASA scientists harnessed the explosive fire that launched us to the moon. Richard not only talked a blue streak, he became one.

Unfortunately, Pryor never did compete in the Olympics (they don't just test for steroids, you know). But he did take fire a long way in a record amount of time—and left the scorch marks in the road to prove it.

Richard Pryor, the marketing genius behind the sizzling designer fragrance, *Halon Pour Hommes*, and a torch of inspiration in this dark and unenlightened world, was born on this date in 1940.

Negation:
Wait 'til you see what I can do with hair-in-a-can. Got a match?

> Richard Gere and Cindy Crawford—he's elastic and she's plastic.
>
> —Sandra Bernhard

Richard Gere and Cindy Crawford, whose 1991 marriage created the world's shallowest gene pool (but what a reflection!), announced their separation on December 2, 1994. Gere and Crawford, who described the split as a "personal and painful decision," prepared for dissolution the same way less-celebrated divorcing couples do: they equitably divided the household supply of gauze (he needs it for close-ups; she needs it to replace what leeches from her ears); they consulted the Dalai Lama on the intricacies of karmic debt buyout; and they took out the customary $30,000 full-page ad in the London *Times* to tell the world that they are not gay.

Negation:

To anyone who knows anything about interior design, it is painfully obvious that we're not gay.

People say conversation is a lost art; how often I have wished it were.

—Edward R. Murrow

We have read that only 15% of regular sinners (the percentage is even lower for irregular sinners) go to confession. God's maitre d's are wondering why. We aren't. Confession has come out of the closet (or whatever you call that telephone booth where it's always too dark to find the directory). Everyone lucky enough to have accumulated a soulful of sins—original and otherwise—has confessed them all already . . . to anyone who will listen.

Want to know who's taken to wearing their spouse's underpants? Hit a wedding. Come garter time, you may even see them. And if you've got a hankering to hear about prolapsed body parts over a platter of chicken liver pâté? Then a baby shower is the place for you. Unfortunately, there's only one place to go to find out why everybody in the family looks so much like Grandpa: the annual reunion.

Special note to Doreen's husband, Tom: You're right. We can't look you in the face. We know where it's been.

Negation:

If you need me, I'll be the sullen one in the corner.

All religions die of one disease; that is, being found out.
                                                    —Christopher Morley

The second session of the Ecumenical Council came to an end in Rome on December 4, 1963. Although Vatican II left many intriguing church mysteries intact (like the exact latitude and longitude of Limbo and whether or not nuns really do have hair), the Council demystified the Mass by, to put it in plain English, putting it in plain English.

The use of understandable language coincidentally coincided with the most dramatic drop ever in church attendance.

Negation:
When I heard the mass in English I became a born-again believer in dead languages. Anything my mind can grasp isn't worth reaching for.

I'd rather have a free bottle in front of me than a prefrontal lobotomy.

—Tom Waits

With the possible exceptions of Rosemary Kennedy and Frances Farmer, wouldn't we all?

Prohibition was repealed on this date in 1933.

— Negation: —

Today I will celebrate the fact that I not only have the intelligence to see that the glass is half empty, but the foresight to ask for another round.

Oh, bummer.

—Jerry Garcia arriving at Altamont

Woodstock is mythologized as the free be-in of the hippie nation rather than the unsuccessful commercial enterprise it actually was. Altamont, on the other hand, *was* a free concert. And the ultimate proof that you get what you pay for.

On this night in the last month of the 1960s, skinflint concert promoters in Altamont, California, destroyed a Rolling Stones-Jefferson Airplane freebie by hiring members of the Hell's Angels (the Manson family was previously booked . . . by the LAPD) to provide security. A group that routinely shares women but reacts inappropriately when its Harleys are mounted, the Hell's Angels beat the audience back from the stage with pool cues, stabbed a man to death, frightened Mick Jagger (something a world full of mirrors couldn't do), and brought down the curtain on the sixties myth of peace and love.

───── Negation: ─────
Is *that* what happened to Taj Mahal's teeth? Bummer.

A date which will live in infamy . . .

—Franklin Delano Roosevelt

December 7, Pearl Harbor Day, lived in infamy from 1941 until the 1980s when America surrendered unconditionally to the need for Japanese VCRs, cars, cameras, microwaves, computers, calculators, copiers, stereos, video game systems, fax machines, and televisions.

You, however, will live in infamy until every member of your third-grade class—and anyone else who might remember that you couldn't "hold it" until the class got back from the field trip to "Waltzing Waters"—surrenders to senility.

Negation:

Twenty-five people who aren't sure whether Pearl Harbor was an act of war or an act they saw in a Vegas taproom remember every infamous detail of my embarrassing childhood.

> Between the conception
> And the creation
> Between the emotion
> And the response
> Falls the Shadow
>   Life is very long
>
> —T. S. Eliot, *The Hollow Men*

So is December a month that groans on like a four-trimester pregnancy.

Of course, there are many incomparable moments to anticipate during this jolly season of salesmanship. You wait for the snowy evening the children send their dreams and their love to Santa . . . and the bleak morning Santa sends the bills to you. You anticipate the day you splurge on something really special for someone you love . . . and the moment of horror when you discover that your loved one has reciprocated with a Garden Weasel— a gift that, for some reason, made her think of you.

Most of all, you look forward to the moment when the last gift is unwrapped, revealing itself to be less magical than it appeared in the commercial. Sure, it casts a pall on the post-Nativity festivities. But the anticipation's over.

Negation:

I'm old enough to know that there are only two kinds of Christmas gifts— the kind I don't want and the kind I don't get.

Health nuts are going to feel stupid someday, lying in
hospitals dying of nothing.

–Redd Foxx

How do I get to Forest Lawn Cemetery without feeling
stupid? Practice, practice. Hey, it worked for Redd Foxx,
star of TV's *Sanford and Son* and the only celebrity
known to have rehearsed for the hearse. Unwilling to be
caught off guard in the event that his life was unexpectedly canceled, Foxx had the "big one" every week
for five seasons on his hit sitcom. When the sixty-eight-
year-old comic finally felt he had gotten it right, he did
it for real on October 11, 1991, on the set of his new
series, *The Royal Family*. Not only did Redd Foxx die of
something, he died of something he was good at.

Redd Foxx was born John Elroy Sanford, son of Fred
Sanford, on this date in 1922. For all we know, that was
just a dry run, too.

Negation:
Death is bad enough without it being a surprise and an embarrassment.

Because I could not stop for Death—
He kindly stopped for me—
The carriage held but just Ourselves—
And Immortality.

—Emily Dickinson

Miss Dickinson was born on this date in 1830. The most celebrated agoraphobic never to appear on a popular talk show, she lived like a mildew in her parents' Amherst, Massachusetts, home where she dedicated her life and great lyric talent to leaving the morbidly depressed loners of this world a body of words to die by.

Of course, her verses lose some of their haunting intensity once some cretin points out that every one of her morose stanzas can be sung to the decidedly upbeat tune of "The Yellow Rose of Texas." If you didn't already know this fun fact, we are proud to be those cretins.

Negation:

Altogether now: *Success is counted sweetest / By those who ne'er succeed...*

I'd rather rot on my own floor than be found by a bunch of bingo players in a nursing home.
—*Florence King, With Charity Toward None*

Several 7000-year-old skulls with brains virtually intact were discovered by archaeologists in Florida on December 11, 1984. The oldest skulls from which it had thus far been possible to extract DNA, they were found buried at the bottom of a lake.

Negation:

Sinkhole, Schminkhole...I'm not going anywhere until that putz calls G-52.

I hope the next time she's crossing the street, four blind guys come along driving cars.

— Frank Sinatra on Kitty Kelly, author of the best-selling *My Way*

He also hopes that the next time he sings in public four deaf guys are writing the reviews.

Ol' teleprompter eyes was born in Hoboken, New Jersey, in 1915.

Negation:
I hope Frank's "blind" friends don't know *my* address.

> Questioning is not the mode of conversation among gentlemen.
>
> —Samuel Johnson

Such thoughts obviously died soon after Johnson himself (on this date in 1784).

Questioning may not be the mode of conversation among gentlemen, but it's certainly the preferred mode of discourse among spokesmodels and other members of genus *Bimbo*. I was born in 1979? Most people don't understand that modeling is really hard work? You have to let your mind go completely empty and not blink for seconds at a time? My agent told me he wasn't happy with my latest layout? I had to get right down on the floor and try it again? I've had breast implants? Not silicone? but with the useless tissue they Hoovered out from between my ears? I have a book deal for a collection of inspirational thoughts? and I just signed a movie contract? But someday I'd really like to produce? Maybe a calendar? Or a couple of kids for Richard Gere?

Negation:

What do you call Ed McMahon with a spokesmodel on each arm? An interpreter?

And there shall in that time be rumours of things going astray, and there will be a great confusion as to where things really are, and nobody will really know where lieth those little things with the sort of raffia work base, that has an attachment, they will not be there. At this time a friend shall lose his friend's hammer and the young shall not know where lieth the things possessed by their fathers that their fathers put there only just the night before . . .

—The Boring Prophet, Monty Python's *Life of Brian*

Nostradamus (Michel de Nostredame), who was born in Saint-Rémy, France, on December 14, 1503, did not divine the single most cultural cataclysm of our time: the popularization of faux marbling among home owners with more available walls than available talent. But he did know this much: obscurity is to the prophet what orange smog is to the otherwise undistinguished skyline of the city of Los Angeles.

Consequently, Nostradamus' poetic quatrains—written in the latest dead language, French—have been stretched to predict everything from the rise of the Ayatollah Khomeini to the daring rescue of Thurston Howell from Gilligan's Island.

Negation:

The prophet will make faces like a prophet.

The angels will speak as with angels' tongues.

The moth will flutter to the light like a moth to the light.

The barn door will be open like a barn door.

(Peter Handke, *Prophecy*)

Psychoanalysis is the mental illness it purports to cure.
                                                    –Karl Kraus

On December 15, 1973, the American Psychiatric Association overturned a 100-year-old position and spontaneously "cured" at least 10% of its own membership by announcing that homosexuality is not a mental illness. They did, however, make a special provision for Rollerina.

Negation:

Today, homosexuality. Tomorrow, that quirky little thing I do…well, that *many* people do…with the, you know, the vacuum cleaner.

Your ancestors—yes, they were a hard lot; but nevertheless, they gave us religious liberty to worship as they required us to worship, and political liberty to vote as the
church required.

—Mark Twain, Speech to a group of *Mayflower* descendants

The national myth holds up this date in 1620 (along
with December 21, 22, and 26 . . . choose the date that
fits in best between polo chukkers) as the day the *Mayflower* ended its monthlong hesitation along the Massachusetts coast, tied up at Plymouth Rock, and disgorged
its homely cargo of English spiritual freedom seekers.
Among the varied and indisputably enriching religious
institutions founded by this notoriously hard lot are
Banking, Cotillionism, the Church of Fundamental Supe-
riority, the Land Rover's Witnesses, the Seventh-Day-
Oh-Drat-the-Maid-Is-Off Lamentists, the Friends-Who-
Live-In-Greenwich, and the Church of the Latter-Day Bor-
dello Madams.

Negation:

I am free to worship at the secular shrine of my choice. My church
doesn't even give Green Stamps.

Man won't fly for a thousand years.

—Wilbur Wright, 1901

Today's the anniversary of the Wright brothers' first flight at Kitty Hawk, North Carolina, in 1903. Orville flew the 750-pound, twelve-horsepower craft first, traveling about 120 feet in twelve seconds. Buoyed by a rising sense of doom and exhilarated by the limitlessness of his own impossibilities, Wilbur promptly broke his brother's record, flying the heavier-than-air machine 825 feet in fifty-nine seconds.

Negation:

You can't keep a chronically un-uplifted man down.

Drugs just accelerate what's going to happen anyway.
—Keith Richards

The biggest surprise to emerge from the sixties and seventies was a living, breathing Keith Richards. He's still alive and in his fifties as this is written, and today he's probably celebrating yet another birthday while there are millions of people in his generation who suffered to watch their diets and drug intakes yet are long gone.

Negation:

The vices I have given up were not the ones that were going to kill me;
the vices I don't know I have are the ones that will.

Benjamin Franklin did a great many notable things for his country . . . It is not the idea of this memoir to ignore that or cover it up. No; the simple idea of it is to snub those pretentious maxims of his, which he worked up with a great show of originality out of truisms that had become wearisome platitudes as early as the dispersion from Babel.

–Mark Twain, *The Late Benjamin Franklin*

Benjamin Franklin was a statesman, printer, scientist, and declaration signer. He was also a writer best known for his jaunty platitudes, like "Early to bed and early to rise will make a man healthy, wealthy, and wise," a piece of wisdom we all wish Conan O'Brien would follow.

On December 19, 1732, Franklin began publishing *Poor Richard's Almanac*. Although it is a matter of some curiosity why anyone would take advice from a man who couldn't even figure out that a pageboy does not flatter a bald spot, the publication flourished. It also set off a 250-year plague of advice books from unlikely sources such as Horatio Alger ("Early to bed and early to rise, work like a dog at a job you despise"), L. Ron Hubbard ("Early to bed and early to rise, you can be a Scientologist if your bankbook's the right size"), and Barbara DeAngelis ("Early to bed and early to rise, I married Doug Henning and four other guys").

Negation:

Early to rise and early to bed makes a man healthy, wealthy and dead.

(James Thurber)

When someone is coming down with egomania, there must be symptoms that an alert diagnostician can spot: model-dating, maybe, or cosmetic surgery, or a tendency to name things after oneself.

–Calvin Trillin, *Diseases of the Mighty*

Landlord to the loathsome and chronic affluenza sufferer Donald Trump clinched two out of three in the symptomatology sweepstakes when he married model-cum-potential-paternity-suit Marla Maples on December 20, 1993. In his defense, at least Donald Trump married a mannequin with depth equal to his own. Upon meeting television castaway Tina Louise, Marla Maples Trump reportedly enthused, *"I'm so excited to meet you. I've always modeled myself after Ginger."*

Negation:

If Donald Trump *has* had cosmetic surgery, he should sue.

Winter is icummen in,
Lhude sing Goddamm,
Raineth drop and staineth slop,
And how the wind doth ramm!
          Sing: Goddamm.
Skiddeth bus and sloppeth us,
An ague hath my ham.
Freezeth river, turneth liver,
          Damn you, sing: Goddamm.
Goddamm, Goddamm, 'tis why I am, Goddamm,
          So 'gainst the winter's balm.
Sing goddamm, damm, sing Goddamm,
Sing goddamm, sing goddamm, DAMM.

          —*Ezra Pound, Ancient Music*

There's less sunlight today than any other day of the year. On the downside, the days will be getting longer and longer from now until June. You'll just have to fight the invigorating effects of more daylight.

Negation:
Goddamm.

Golf is not a sport. Golf is men in ugly pants walking.
                                              —Rosie O'Donnell

On December 22, 1894, representatives of five golf clubs from New York, Massachusetts, Rhode Island, and Chicago frittered away a day too cold for a quick nine by forming the United States Golf Association (USGA). The Association guaranteed golfers (a highly visible minority) many rights, including the right to wear pink and green plaid pants and ride around in funny little cars without ever actually becoming Shriners.

——————— *Negation:* ———————
I can lose my balls without paying a greens fee.

Awards are like hemorrhoids; in the end, every asshole
gets one.

–Frederic Raphael

Perennial Miss Demeaniality and over-rehearsed gra-
cious loser Susan Lucci has been nominated exactly ump-
teen times for a daytime Emmy Award she did not win.
An actress who set the tone for her career as a runner-
up in the New York State Miss Universe pageant, Lucci
finally got what was rightfully hers on _____ . (Fill
in the blank with the inevitable date.)

Ashes ashes we all fall down
                    —Traditional lyrics to the children's symbolic dance of death

Billionaire Howard Hughes took his first gasp of air in Houston, Texas (arguably the same air gasped by those born on this date in the slums of Calcutta), on this the eve of the Feast of Greed, in 1905. As dashing and enigmatic as only a limitless pile of greenbacks can make one, the "reclusive" Hughes made aviation history in 1938 by flying around the world in the then record time of three days, nineteen hours, and fourteen minutes. He is most fondly remembered, however, for growing the world's longest fingernails and still being able to change the channel on the fuzzy television in the tacky motel room where he died.

Negation:
He who dies with the most toys, dies.

> 'Peace upon earth!' was said. We sing it,
> And pay a million priests to bring it.
> After two thousand years of mass
> We've got as far as poison-gas.
>
> —Thomas Hardy, *Christmas: 1924*

Of course, weapons technology has progressed even further since Hardy penned the snappy carol that's always been a family favorite at our house. Nuclear missile silos still dot the world's landscape in greater numbers than the currently politically incorrect neighborhood crèches.

More optimistic authors might point out to you on this day of peace and goodwill toward men (and we do mean *men*; women will be too busy working in the kitchen), that the weapons of mass destruction are now being dismantled. Knowledge, however, is a funny thing. It can't be dismantled or even buried for a thousand years in a concrete bunker. It can only be stockpiled, like the wallets, handkerchiefs, and bottles of cologne of Christmases past that molder in the back of your sock drawer. Until, in case of emergency, you need to pull it out again.

Negation:
Maybe the Pentagon could find some use for that stockpile of English Leather I've been hoarding since 1972.

Fighting is the only racket where you're almost guaranteed to end up as a bum.

–Rocky Graziano

It's Boxing Day in Britain. All we Americans really know about it is that it's somebody else's paid holiday (Yes, everyone in the world *does* get more holidays and vacation days than you do, but if it makes you feel better, remember that holidays in many exotic locales are accompanied by fasting and hostage-taking and female circumcision and other discomfiting pursuits).

As far as we can figure out, Boxing Day is either the day set aside for boxing up the mounds of Christmas garbage and putting it out with the dustbins, or it's the day you start slugging it out with the relatives who have outlasted the eggnog, outlived the Christmas tree, and are now settling in for a long winter's nap in a bed that used to be yours. We like the latter theory. It gives us a chance to ruminate on the only sport that has a major mental disorder—*dementia pugilistica*—named after it. If, for some strange reason, Christmas hasn't depressed you sufficiently this year, then take a minute trying to reconcile your earliest memory of Cassius Clay with your most recent image of Muhammad Ali.

Negation:
And take your orthopedic Christmas stocking with you.

There should be PMS shelters for men.

—Jeff Foxworthy

Your local spit-on-the-floor tavern may offer free pay-per-view and chloroform masks on "hyperventilation night," but history has shown that it offers no protection from abrupt swings of temperament . . . or even hatchets.

On December 27, 1900, Carry Nation, quite possibly in the post-chocolate letdown phase of her menstrual cycle, staged her first big raid as a prohibitionist. She marched into a saloon in the basement of the Carey Hotel in Wichita, Kansas, and shrieked her disgust at the patrons. Then she smashed all the liquor bottles she could reach with her famous hatchet. Before she left, she stopped to throw rocks at a nude painting of Cleopatra above the bar—the turn-of-the-century version of a wide-screen TV playing the Howard Stern New Year's Eve Party.

Negation:
I blame my hormones for everything.

Gaiety

Gaiety is the most outstanding feature of the Soviet Union.

—Joseph Stalin

And Joseph Stalin was the Wink Martindale of his time. To prove it, Alexander Solzhenitsyn published *The Gulag Archipelago* on this date in 1973, a book which detailed the secret funza-poppin' party games that made Soviet prison life under Stalin so gay.

Among the pleasant diversions he described were "Let's-get-you-wet-and-stand-you-outside-for-a-few-hours" (a favorite in Siberia), the popular and challenging "I-know-the-ground-is-frozen-but-go-dig-a-five-mile-long-pit-just-for-the-heck-of-it" game, and the ultimate test of endurance and the inspiration for the long-running "Truth or Consequences": "How-long-can-you-live-in-a-hole-in-the-ground-on-three-and-a-half-ounces-of-bread-a-day?"

Shortly thereafter, Solzhenitsyn was expelled from the Soviet Union and forced to live in a much less stimulating place: Vermont.

Negation:

No wonder fifteen five-year-olds laughed in my face when I suggested they play "Pin-the-Tail-on-the-Donkey" at my kid's party.

I find it no more dangerous than the martini . . . I have every night before dinner. I would like to see that law loosened.

> —Mary Tyler Moore on the all-natural alternative to a "nothing day": pot

Mary Tyler Moore, who turned the world on with her smile, was born on December 29, 1936.

I feel that I shall leave life before January 1.
—Grigory Yefimovich Rasputin

Rasputin, graduate of the Nostradamus school of profound obscurity, certainly sounded the part of the mystic. But this time the mad monk was on to something. His hell-bound troika *was* scheduled to leave before the new year. And it took many tries to get him on board.

On the evening of December 30, 1917, Prince Felix Yussupov and Vladimir Purishkevich, in a lavish display of Russian hospitality, offered Rasputin some cakes laced with potassium cyanide. Rasputin gulped them down without suffering so much as an abdominal cramp. The assassins followed up with a poisoned Madeira chaser. It didn't even slow Rasputin down. Now desperate, Yussupov shot him in the back. Rasputin was down long enough to be declared dead, yet he made a break for it and got two more bullets for his trouble. Though the mystic fell, he was still alive enough to grind his teeth.

That's when Yussupov and Purishkevich decided it would be curtains for him. They beat Rasputin with a steel rod, wrapped his body in a window drape, and stuffed the package through a hole in the ice into the Neva River. When Rasputin's body was discovered three days later, his lungs were full of water. The mad monk of Siberia was finally dead . . . from drowning.

Negation:

I'll think twice before I join the New Year's revelers in Times Square.

Woman at a dance: *Oh, Mr. Shaw, what made you ask poor little me to dance?*

George Bernard Shaw: *Well, this is a charity ball, isn't it?*

Every year since 1954, just before New Year's Day, the unremarkable offspring of unhyphenated Americans gather in the Grand Ballroom of New York's Waldorf-Astoria for the International Debutante Ball. An event characterized by wretched excess (One patrician papa popped for ten thousand Brazilian butterflies which he kept, netted, a bit too close to the ceiling lights. When he released them in his daughter's honor, he showered the revelers with their corpses.), the Debutante Ball is nevertheless a bona fide charitable event, providing dance partners for the congenitally rhythmless, an avenue of presentation for the unpresentable, and suitably inbred husbands for the otherwise unsuitably inbred debs.

----- *Negation:* -----

My parents spent every cent they had on a fancy coming-out ball for me, but I haven't had the holes drilled in it yet.

Index of Topics

❖ ❖ ❖

Those of you too impatient to wait weeks or months until your favorite subject is covered might want to use this list of 366 topics to choose your own meditation for the day.

368